Joe approaches automotive sales and the F&I process with a "punch-you-in-the-gut" brutal honesty! He holds nothing back as he openly shares the challenges he experienced in this business and the mental, emotional, and practical skills he developed that shaped and forged him into a top-producing F&I manager. You should read this book if you are a person wanting to understand the psychological process you and your customer go through and that you must be able to master in order to achieve all of the success you desire and deserve. He includes over 70 immediately implementable and relevant closes that every F&I manger must be equipped with so that you can offer the highest value to your clients and retain the most profitability for you dealership. I strongly endorse and recommend this book to anyone who wants to think outside the box about ways to be more productive and profitable "in the box"!

Jonathan Dawson
Founder of Sellchology – Selling through psychology
Automotive Sales Trainer | Consultant | Speaker | Author

76 Cash Making, Deal Saving Closes

A Guide to Selling Cars, Extended
Warranties and Service Contracts

By
Joe Sabatini

76 Cash Making, Deal Saving Closes

*A Guide to Selling Cars,
Extended Warranties and Service Contracts*

by Joe Sabatini
Copyright © 2017 Joe Sabatini
Published by SkillBites LLC
All rights reserved.

ISBN-10:1-942489-28-5
ISBN-13:978-1-942489-28-3

Acknowledgements

I'd like to acknowledge some of my mentors. First, Rick Hauk for taking a shot on me when just about everybody else wouldn't. To be provided the opportunity to pick myself up while being part of your team is something I will never forget and this very book would have never been thought of if I never went back "in the box."

Second, my very first mentor in the car business, Bill Mears, for without his belief in my ability to use my weaknesses as strengths, I don't know how I would've wound up in sales. A truly inspirational manager. I evaluate myself comparatively to his abilities daily in terms of trying to find an ounce of greatness in all of my sales guys.

Last but not least, a man that has fired me but I still love the guy to death, Mr Michael Freeman and also the best closer I've ever met, Gokhan Seker at Main Line Honda. True masters of persistence in closing!

I'd also like to acknowledge my sources of education: Monsignor Bonner High School in Drexel Hill, PA, for encouraging me to speak and act in accordance to whatever it is that my will dictates regardless of how uncomfortable (or how much trouble) I got in. But also, that my will should include loving all people, even those that hate me. A truly encouraging place to become a man!

Delaware County Community College and Peirce College for my further education which has intrinsically propelled me to evolve, adapt and persist by learning about myself, people and the marketplace.

Dedication

To my father, a true gentleman but also the quintessence of what it means to be a real man. The greatest teacher I have in life because he taught me that it's manners that truly make the man; that it's of no nobility whatsoever to attempt to compare yourself in superiority to that of other men; and that it is of utmost gentlemanly greatness to always attempt to be greater than one's previous self.

To the Tomasetti's, Paganos, Ciarlantes, Diegnans, DiNardis' and Cassel Families, and to the entire Woods Family, especially, Albert, Kevin and John. The Original Wolf Pack! From my childhood until present, your families have always been there for me to make sure that giving up is never an option.

Table of *Contents*

I

Introduction and Overview

$\mathcal{P}$reface

Reality

I know the people in the car business are incredibly busy so I wanted to make a point to let the reader know that you can see significant improvements just reading the chapter on Closes. I can relate and totally understand as I have about 4 books that I've gotten three quarters of the way through and I really do want to finish, but I can't for some reason. So, please if getting the best use of it means using the closes only, then start there and see how you feel about them when you're trying them out.

Personal Experience and Influences

I've been in the automobile business since 2005 and I am surprised by the disparate success rate of the salespeople. It's the first thing about the business that intimidated, perplexed and awed me to the point where I needed to find out why. Why was there this big difference? Why is it that amongst sales people (many who work extra-long hours, 55 – 60 a week) there is such a disparity of income? In this business, it was possible for a guy to have a summer house, three cars, expensive suits, Rolexes and all the excesses a skilled professional can have. I also saw salespeople moping around the showroom, talking about other salespeople and muttering comments like, "the boss hooks them up," and "they get all the leads," etc. I became friendly with people at both ends of the spectrum as is my habit and as a rookie I listened to both.

From day one I feared becoming inefficient. I feared coming to work and owing the company money as a result. I learned the hard way. Although I feared it, I was unable to avoid the shadow of despair and self-doubt. I began blaming customers for their lack of logic because I couldn't sell them and I brought home such meager paychecks. I found all kinds of ways to excuse my lack of success. So, I often changed dealerships because the customers were better somewhere else, the banks weren't buying deep enough, the product wasn't good enough, etc. Also, when the successful guys were ringing up sales it would anger me to a point of helplessness – as if I would never be like them.

You may wonder how I got myself out of that shadow? You may be thinking: *What made him stay in this business that he was having little to no success in?* The best advice I will ever give to any reader is persistence. Even when you're failing, if you keep your mind open, you will learn to be successful. Even if you're failing, you can and will progress to success over time. Your efforts are not wasted because you can (or should) learn something from every failure. I know it's the new cliché: "Don't give up, man! I'm never ever gonna give you up," you hear in the voice of the singer

Barry White. Truth is, persistence was required mentally and physically – but it was really all mental. The question then becomes: "How do you persist mentally?" Through many mistakes, I've discovered a much more efficient way of persisting that can save the reader jobs and money. Also, I've seen many instances of building things up on one day, just to tear them down the next out of frustration. I will say that (and I can't even believe I'm saying it) education, reading and keeping up with the things that I enjoyed has improved my stress threshold, demeanor and professionalism immensely.

Who needs a Gun, When You Were Born to Master the Art of Persuasion?

The question is calling to all the people who have found themselves in sales. It's calling for people that have failed and yet try again and again with the most powerful tools you have at your disposal: Hope and Faith (they're not just the names of strippers at your local dance club).

My real history is one of resilience. I was born with an innately fast temper and choleric state of mind, that at times still gets me in trouble to this day but I've come a long way. I grew up in Philadelphia playing some form of hockey up until I was about 30 and I always got into fights during hockey and sometimes in life. These fights made my nose look like something out of a stereotypical witch's costume, which then led me into (you guessed it) more fights. As soon as somebody even hinted at making fun of my nose, I went off and fast! One of my displays of anger nearly cost me my life when, to keep it short, events occurred that led me to smashing my hand through a glass window. My entire left hand was rendered useless. The emergency surgeons called it a "spaghetti wrist" because the glass cut through all my tendons, arteries and nerves. Life gets pretty interesting when you see blood literally squirting out of your arm; not only that, but I was born left handed.

It was at this point my life began! I lost everything that meant anything to me: my career in law enforcement, my girlfriend, my money and my direction all gone. The doctors told me that I would never have normal use of my hand again.

That is when I learned how to use my anger as fuel and productivity. I decided I was going to insist on making the first change of my life at 25 years old. I realized I didn't have to be the way "I always was." I realized that "genetics" or being "a hot-tempered Italian" didn't predetermine my life and the choices yet to be made. I realized that I chose what to accept as impossible day in and day out.

I started my first sales job, with one hand. I learned to write with my right hand on the job. I learned to button a shirt and pants with one hand. I learned to ask for help because I couldn't do some things, like lift or feel my hands (I still can't feel parts of my left hand to this day) and I realized that I had a major flaw in not asking people (and life in general) for enough. I wasn't asking enough of myself either.

Put your guns down. Let me say it again. Put your guns down and realize that you need to enjoy the ride of life with persuasion! If you have an angry customer, disarm him with charm and sell him or her on how little of a deal a transaction will ultimately mean to them over the course of their life. A customer that you cannot agree on terms with? Make them realize the value with a smile and let them know that they've already won. Most importantly, be genuinely honored by the people that visit you, as if they were your favorite idol. Let your guard down. Do not look to justify anger or injustice to find blame. Why? Because, in sales, what does it matter?

You want to be right? Great! You're right, but you failed to make the connection with the customer. You're right. The customer is an asshole, so you don't need to follow up with him…but another salesperson is now going to get *your commission*. Let me ask, how does it feel to be so right? Do not seek to be righteous, rather seek to persuade with a close based on the strength of common ground and mutual respect.

Always seek to find the good in others. Always accept the challenge of somebody you think may be superior in knowledge or negotiation skill because you won't learn how to negotiate from people that are less effective than you. Make allowances for things that are not fair and move on with life. If you need to look at it from a different perspective, allow yourself to be humble and patient enough to find the human being in a person that disagrees with you, even if they do so vociferously. Like I said before, just focus on enjoying the ride first.

I salute anybody that has the courage to wake up, day in and day out, on full commission and not have a clue if their 12-hour workday will yield any income. I know men who fought wars that wouldn't face a commission only job. So be proud and believe in your mental toughness. In sales, always look for ways to emulate the best. Ask yourself, "What would the greatest salesperson I've ever met do to persuade and close?"

The Reality Check for Salespeople

In these times, people are quick to anger and even quicker to judge. Be the person who stands out as a sign in the opposite direction, especially *for yourself.* How many people have sold themselves self-cynicism, self-defeat, or impossibility? How quick are we to act as both judge and jury regarding *our inability?* How quickly did we take "no" for an answer? How prepared were we to serve our customers? What excuses do you come up with to stay in your comfort zone, in which "the bubble" protects you and you are always right? Do you want to be right about mediocrity? Mediocrity is the unsafe zone – even worse than failing because at least if you fail, you can move on with life or try something different, but mediocrity, like gravity, keeps you "stuck" right where you are.

How Should I Persist?

Anybody who knows how to spell can simply sit here and say, "Just don't quit." Right? Of course. But what are the machinations of persistence? What is it that will automatically spur you to take productive action when the temptation and evil (yes, evil) of loathing and self-pity enters your mind? The first thing I recommend (and probably the easiest thing as well) is to become inspired by the most successful people around you. That's right. Drop the ego down to earth for one second and humble yourself and befriend a great! The most successful people are always willing to take five minutes to explain themselves. Trust me, one thing successful people like talking about is themselves and how they're so – relatively – successful.

Secondly, learn what to ignore – on the inside and out. You must view yourself as somebody who will make an impact. You will persist until you succeed. Repeat that mentally to yourself 100 times every day and watch what happens when you feel like giving up. You will convert the "No" into a "Yes." For your own mental health, be selfish when it comes to demanding the best effort from yourself. Be willing to fail, and you will find the paths to success because you will learn what didn't work; you will learn what you "could've said" or what you will "try on the next one," and you will discover mental paths to getting that

"Yes." But you must fully exert yourself mentally. Like I said, be selfish about it!

Lastly, become obsessed: with closing, with word tracks, with spending all the extra time that is necessary above and beyond what is required. Are you willing to spend time after work? Are you willing to make the extra phone calls? Are you willing to listen to the most cynical of customers and understand why you may have failed to meet their needs of certainty, trust and confidence?

When we set consistent goals, there is always a fear of not achieving them. That, however, is one of the many reasons why you need to bend failures to your benefit. Furthermore, understand that after each successive "No" you hear, the next "Yes" is inevitably closer. Make it a habit of never forgetting that the next "Yes" will come, even in the hardest of slumps.

Be in Control. Make the Decision on WHAT you want to feel

So many times, I hear about sales slumps, a-hole customers that won't listen to anything the salespeople are saying, negative moods, dealerships that suck, pay plans that suck, successful sales people manipulating the system, management feeding everyone but me, "wwwwhhhhaaa, wwhhhaaa, wwwwhhhaaaaa."

Ladies and gentlemen, the worst mistake a salesperson can make is to prequalify a customer because once you do that you create a self-fulfilling prophecy that satisfies your ego and inner need to be right about the fact that you actually have no control. It's very easy to rationalize and justify because it's easy to produce excrement. Excuses and complaints are the mental junk food that lead to failure Sorry to be frank, but that's the plain truth.

I was having an episode like this one day on the sales floor and I literally thank God every day that somebody cared enough to teach me humility in a mentoring and caring way. His name was Bill; he was my manager at a Honda store in Delaware County, Pennsylvania. I started going off about how: "All of these f%$$##@ customers are f^&*** assholes! I can't get them to buy ***, this place sucks, these customers suck, blah, blah." I had my mind made up that I was not responsible for my lack of success.

Unfortunately, most people believe the same thing! It serves that tiny little piece of greatness that your ego justifies, and you may feel that you must maintain and hold onto firmly what is simply a bad habit or pattern. So, if you're a below average salesperson (5-7 cars a month) or a below average finance manager at 30-40% warranty penetration, you need to repeat this sentence out loud and listen to what a disservice your ego is doing to the real you: "I am the greatest 5 car a month (or 30% warranty penetration finance manager) ever!" Seriously, say it out loud and hopefully you'll only feel embarrassed by yourself because the truth is the statement and the results are hilariously embarrassing. After you pick up the pieces of your ego laying on the ground, look at yourself in the mirror and take responsibility for your performance.

Understand that all those rejections are meant to expand your capabilities. The human psyche creates a need for stability that is a constant hindrance to change in any way – whether it's good or bad! So, if you find yourself uncomfortable at the thought of changing, I suggest you don't mentally hide from it. Seek the truth through other people you know who are more successful than you. Ask what they do, how they do it and (most importantly) how they grew into themselves. You need to commit to never taking the easy way out. You must think about changing because your mind needs to acknowledge that the lack of challenge is a warning sign that you will not succeed.

Back to my story about how I was positively mentored. Bill took me by the collar. Bear in mind I'm 6'1." He dragged me in front of the mirror and said, "You know who the asshole is?"

I looked down, disgusted, trying to laugh it off and said, "Ok, Bill, let me go."

He repeated, "Do you know who the asshole is?"

At this point I knew he wasn't going to let me off the hook, so I looked at him, swallowed my pride and then looked in the mirror. Finally, I said, "I'm the asshole."

"That's right," Bill said. "You're the asshole that refuses to change your mind about actually selling yourself, the car and overcoming objections."

Sounds simple, or harsh, but it worked and I immediately realized that I create my own weather. I have the power to look at hard work as an opportunity to succeed, to sell that notoriously tough Asian customer, the guy who has been to fifty dealerships. Suddenly, I was willing and able to tackle these customers with confidence – initially, for no other reason than I decided I was going to create a mood of appreciation and not give power to the negative sales experiences I usually had. The negative experiences should only be recalled to create new closes. The best way to do this is to reflect on how the best salesperson in the world would handle it. Easier yet, ask the best salespeople on your floor, and they'll tell you. As a matter of fact, I considered the problems as "the gifts." I became obsessively thoughtful about what I could do better the next time.

In life, you have a choice to utilize your memories as a source of strength or the cause for why the world is always handing you a shit sandwich. I'm not going to say that life never does this because it does, but you still have the ability to nullify it by resisting negative outside influences (the other miserable people), or negative emotions like anger and frustration. Most of us have such imbedded patterns that we often forget to realize that we have a choice on how to feel and what "weather" we will bring to our customers, to our relationships, to our problems. Your mental state has body language, voice tonality differences that everyone picks up on. Body language is read more accurately by human beings than words coming out of your mouth. Therefore, feeling inspired will change your voice, your body language, your thought patterns and your self-talk. Remember to make it a habit to choose your "emotional verb" consciously and you will look to improve yourself.

When in such a bad mental place, start from the outside in! I know it sounds odd, but scientific studies show that testosterone levels increase significantly just by standing upright and hands on the hips for just three minutes (picture Superman). If you want to be happy, act happy by taking fuller breaths, sitting or standing upright and finding a way to smile (even if you need to take a break and divert your focus temporarily).

I want everybody to make an important choice as it relates to memory because within memory we can derive what's best in us or – unfortunately and maybe habitually – what's worst in us. Extraordinary effort comes from ordinary people who put themselves in their own voluntary situations. So, when we repeat processes within our given situation, we develop patterns, learning habits and most importantly we make decisions about the world from our perspectives. Accord to Dr. Philip Zimbardo, in his book *The Lucifer Effect*, "Memory enables us to profit from mistakes and build upon the known to create better futures. However, with memory comes grudges, revenge, learned helplessness and rumination over trauma that feeds depression." *The Lucifer Effect* is a great book by the way. I highly recommend it to anybody in the sales field to understand human behavior.

Focus on Zimbardo's words. Read them over and over again.

There is an opportunity here to use your memory with ease so let's do that. Memory enables – which means it's on automatic, without effort, like breathing. Use it to profit from mistakes and build upon the known. You build upon the known by continually reading, training and educating yourself to create a better future. It's that easy, people! Put your brain on autopilot for 5-10 minutes after you have an encounter you're not happy with and figure out what tools you're going to use to overcome the negative result in a positive way the next time you're in a similar situation and decide to be confident, courageous and willing to fail again until you get the result you desire. You *will* get the result you desire, I promise you that.

Grudges, anger, hate, loathing, self-loathing and mental beat downs take effort believe it or not. Your brain is actually working harder to feel these ways because these patterns ruminate and create depression and overload. Why make your brain work harder just to find yourself in a pile of your own mental defecation? Live with the pursuit of what you want. Choose it every single second of every day!

Actual Closing Ratios and Why I Wrote This Book

My career in Finance and the Insurance industry started at a Honda store in an affluent suburb of Philadelphia. The one thing most of our customer base had was plenty of cash and security if things went wrong with their vehicles. Needless to say, I had to learn how to sell the actual value of the warranties and various other ancillary products rather than the "fear," or the potential "savings." I struggled profoundly at first. I didn't know how to properly insist on my products comfortably.

Admittedly, even today, I still get a bit nervous at the awkwardness of the silences after the customer rejects my offers. This odd silence is quite normal to feel and trust me, if you've done a proper and professional job at introducing yourself, it's just as uncomfortable for them too. My understanding of body language, buying signals, buying phrases, questions and objections has led me to be at 90% Vehicle Service Contract penetration, 60% GAP penetration and 45 – 50% Tire and Wheel Package Penetration, month in and month out! To sum it up, my ability to face failure – and not shut down mentally – has led me to success ratios unheard of in the auto industry and my only regret is that it took as long as it has for me to get this message to all the Business Managers, Finance and Insurance Managers, Floor and General Managers and also Dealer Principals.

I'm not going to BS anybody out there. I've had days in the beginning that I just felt like crawling into a hole and forgetting I ever signed up for this God awful job! So, if I can overcome the despair I felt, the disappointment of going 0 – for whatever when another finance manager put $20,000 on the books in one day, anybody can! Understand that bad days will pass and so will the good ones. Remember Finance and Insurance is the "Harvard Business School" of the sales world. I sincerely believe that Finance and Insurance Managers are the hardest, most badass and seasoned salespeople alive. What other job does one deal with 8-9 sets of tracked customers and get measured with such scrutiny? The ratios, the compliance, not pissing the customers off when you try to close them 20 times on a warranty, etc.

Let's also face the fact that – as some of the best sales people in the world – we're not going to have great days every day! Did Wayne Gretzky, Michael Jordan, Jerry Rice, Joe Montana, Jack Nicklaus, Mickey Mantle win every game? Did they strike out, get shutout, make bogeys and interceptions? Absolutely! But what separated them from the pack? They never stopped becoming obsessed with perfecting their craft in the face of disappointments and setbacks. We're going to try like hell! It is important to zealously inspect and correct that which enters your mind and if you do become infected with hopelessness and despair what will you do? You will take action! You will not stop! You will bounce back! You will persist until you succeed – even if the day is a failure and when the day is over – whether great or totally crappy – you will bury it. You will not be overconfident with accomplishments of the past nor burdened of the mind to "what could've, should've been." This is the mark of a PROFESSIONAL!

Most importantly, you will never stop reading, training and listening to the geniuses of your craft or of any other for that matter. Isn't success universally known to a great extent? You know it when you hear it, see it, smell it and feel it. Right? Never stop reading and meeting new people and practice the art of going out of your way to see the human ("similar") side of every one you meet. You do enjoy success and reading about that which is successful, right? Speaking of which, go out of your way to read about the start of Aaron Rodgers' career, his story is the infrastructure for what it takes to become great. Make these *your* habits, too.

The Greatest Habit of All!

Before I get to the juicy parts of what you will learn from this book, I want to make a point. An exclamation point, to remember that love is the most important thing you can give to any customer you encounter. Anybody who knows me, knows that I do not go around with this cheesy looking, fake and hippy glow about me as if I live in some fairytale. When I say love, I mean to take action, to listen, compliment and look people in the eye and to yourself say, "The genuine pleasure is all mine" when you meet someone. They cannot resist something about you, I promise, you will make a friend to some extent with a lot of people – a great many more than if you didn't make a conscious point to do this. This paragraph was influenced by *The Greatest Salesman in The World* by Og Mandino. You must read this book. It will literally change your life.

Who Else Can Benefit from (at least) The Closes in This Book
— Outside of the Car Business?

It has to occur to every reader out there, some working for
the companies I'm about to mention: Apple, Dell, Best Buy,
State Farm, Nationwide, Geico, Progressive, LA Fitness/
Trainers, Staples, Lowe, Home Depot, Game Stop, HVAC
Companies, various appliance companies, plumbing
contractors, water companies, Helzberg Diamonds
and other jewelry shops all offer warranties and other
protections. Everybody needs to understand that these are
forms of insurance that provide peace of mind and that "No
matter what, I'm covered," feeling. It's the salesperson's job
to make the customer feel that the price of that feeling is
worth as much or more than the cash price they're paying.
While there are derivatives of other sales tactics in my
closes, all of my closes have that end goal {peace of mind}
that is at the forefront of the customer's mind. I'm sure
that the reader doesn't have to go much further to know
the other persons that this could apply to are the sales
representatives who work at the above-mentioned firms
and firms like them all over the country.

Insurance agents are selling very similar products;
it just happens that a lot of the lines they sell are a
requirement of law. Here's the takeaway for all the
insurance agents reading this. How many of your existing
customers only have the insurance products required
by law? How many have you tried upselling personal
umbrellas to, lower comprehensive, collision deductibles,
higher limits or any other service that increases premiums

19

for your agency? I know there are millions of dollars of premiums just waiting to be spent and luckily for you insurance agents out there, you have a semi-captive long-term customer. They already trust you at least a little bit and you have several opportunities to upsell at later dates.

Along the same lines of insurance agents come the financial advisors and life insurance sales representatives – and the insurance agents should be looking to delve into this pie as well too. The advantage of these huge companies is the diversification of their product portfolios – use them! Leverage them. Do not say "no" for the customer – *just because you would say no yourself.* This is the number one stumbling block of every sales professional – including myself from time to time.

There are a lot of fundamentals with contracts and upgrading that should always be followed in regards to packaging services and closing, regardless of the product. The wording may need to be adapted for your field, but the ideas in closing are universal for the most part. Closing the customer remains the best service you can offer.

If you are closing any service after the initial sale of an HVAC unit, maintenance plan, computer, car insurance, life insurance, iPod, etc., any contract that offers a convenience, discounted rate of maintenance or service for the unforeseen, you can take this info and apply it.

If you are a career manager, salesperson, manager, insurance agent and you think you've heard it all – this book is especially for you because people like you will incorporate at least one of these closes and perfect it. Bruce Lee said, "Do not fear the man that can do 1,000 moves 1 time, but fear the man that can do 1 move 1,000 times!" Repetition is key to perfection!

Consumer Reports: The Biggest Frauds IN THE HISTORY OF ALL FRAUDS

Companies like Consumer Reports, and all these customer advocacy sites, you know what they are doing better than you? SELLING! They are selling the customer that you – the insurance, after – market sales guy/girl – are trying to "rip them off" by selling them products that the consumer may use – at least for their own comfort. Does anybody know why Consumer Reports is doing this? TO MAKE MONEY! Their agenda is no different than ours, my friends. They earn people's trust, respect and loyalty through their subscriptions and magazines (that are marked up hundreds and thousands of percentage points by the way), that advertisers pay for and they *sell*. It's your obligation to deal with these objections head on and get the customer talking about it so you can sell what you believe in and the benefits of it. Do your research. How much does it cost to print a magazine or offer online advice? Think about it. Then ask them what I'm asking you regarding whatever you are selling and you'll find the motive as to why Consumer Reports has a motivation to write for or against it. I will reveal my closes regarding this in Chapter Six. This is not an impossible objection to overcome. Lastly, and most importantly, since when has the American consumer decided that they don't have the confidence, instinct and reasonable train of thought and logic to make a decision based on **all of the information out there**. Since when did Consumer Reports decide that they have the monopoly on influence? Why should any consumer forfeit their right to change – or make up – their own minds? Consumer Reports claims to not have biased motives, but look at the numerous complaints. For example, they charge people without permission – that's unlawful, isn't it? Also, Consumer Reports has teamed up with True Car for their buying service. No bias there? My point is, Consumer Reports has a profit motive to pay themselves and keep renewals up. Their entire revenue seeking model is based on getting you signed up and keeping you for life. Why? More cash! Non-profit companies are able to pay their executives handsomely by law and I can assure you that the top executives are making a lot more money than the car salesman who thinks you should pay an extra $1,000 for an automobile. It's our job to make people see our points logically – as a true benefit to them – and it is your goal to use their time most efficiently by allowing them to open-up their minds and listen. You do this by showing you truly care while talking and speaking with them and allowing your professional, experienced, "having been in the trenches," logic, or "what I've found," and "what I've typically seen" real-life approach overrule some magazine written by an "expert". Keep in mind, this is some guy who works in a cubicle all day, wears nothing but khakis, gets done at 5 p.m. sharp and couldn't care less about anything other than maintaining his/her own job. If you Google "Consumer Reports negative reviews" you'll see the agendas that are already known: Constant bad mouthing of American automobiles, auto renewals without authorizations, dummied down (more cost-efficient) "expert" reviews. Build your case if you believe in what you do to make a living. Do not just accept – without a strong fight – your ability to turn a Consumer Reports advocate into a profitable customer who trusts you and refers all his/her people to you.

There's great news about these Consumer Reports types of people though. That news is they need help making a decision. So, you have to do the things that I will explain later to gain the people's trust so they turn to you for advice. I used to hear salesperson after salesperson complain about the "guy with the Consumer Reports" on the lot. After you read this, you'll be begging for that challenge because you'll have confidence in the tools that will make you successful, assertive and close more deals with more profit.

II

The Professional Demeanor

*"The will to win is not nearly
as important as the will –
to prepare – to win"*

Just in case you were off in space somewhere when you read that the first time, let me repeat it. THE WILL TO WIN IS NOT NEARLY AS IMPORTANT AS THE WILL – TO PREPARE – TO WIN! We all want to be able to storm out of the tunnel in our Notre Dame helmets, New York Yankee stripes and Sylvester Stallone like (or Christie Brinkley like for the females out there) figures, but do we want to be Rudy Ruddiger? Mickey Mantle? Or the Sly Stallone that was literally living out of his car? The answer better be, "Yes" after you complete this paragraph! You must prepare yourself with never ending training and learning. Also, you have to get yourself inspired mentally every day – whatever it takes. Find a way to get yourself in a positive mental place to address every customer as a professional. You need to focus on and be obsessed with your "Why." Who or what are you working for? Where do you want to be? What do you want to be? These are questions that only you – the reader – can answer.

Why?

Because within two seconds – I'll even say within a quarter of a second, your customers completely size you up and make a decision about who you are, whether you're worth listening to, and – most importantly – if they will buy something from you. This may not be fair, but it is true, that appearances mean more than they should and if you're not a professional yet, or you're a green pea, the good news is you can act like you are and people will listen to you based on how you act, how you speak, how you address them with your body language and demeanor, and how you look. So, everything you have within you better be hyper focused and intentionally put forth into making the customer in front of you see you in a positive, comfortable, trustworthy, encouraging and assertive manner. Your goal in F and I is to be cool no matter what the customer objects to or the concerns that they raise.

Body Language, Successful Introduction and Gaining Trust Instantly

The implications of body language are far more important than anything you say. It's psychologically proven that people listen to 90% of what your body is saying and only 10 to 20% to what is actually coming out of your mouth. As I said before, your body language at the initial contact and what you say better be as close to the most comforting, assertive, enthusiastic approach every time. This is easier said than done, simply because your customers' body language may not be the same; as a matter of fact, if they've been waiting a long time, they're ready just to get out of the dealership or store. Right? More on that a little later in the book, but it's important to mentally get the customer up to your level of attention and willingness to be open minded.

So, according to the Wolf of Wall Street, Jordan Belfort, it's important to acknowledge that the customer is interviewing you mentally [primarily] on three separate (KEY) things that will determine if, and how attentively and openly, they will listen to you. One: "Are you sharp as a tack?" Two: "Are you genuinely enthusiastic and glad to see them?" Three: "Are you an expert in your field?" I strongly urge any reader of this book to go onto YouTube, Facebook and Mr. Belfort's website to see what he's doing. I can assure you, you will see why this guy was the best at whatever he was selling. He will inspire you to take yourself to the next level for sure.

"Are you Sharp as a Tack?"

Whether it's personal or professional, everybody is sizing you up. Wherever you go, people want to know what kind of person you are. In the F and I position, the first thing people will immediately want to know is "How important am I, how important is this guy/girl I just met and how much is my business valued?" Your body language, introduction and acknowledgement is the key to answer this question. Right? So, first things first, you make sure you're standing up as the customer walks into your office or as you walk out to them. Your body language is tall and upright; your handshake is firm and there is a warm smile on your face. You look everybody in the eye. I cannot stress the importance of this enough. You look the customer in the eye, with a smile and you say something positive to yourself to make the smile sincere and genuine. Something I learned from *The Greatest Salesman in the World* is to look people in the eye and say, "I love you" to them under your breath. I know, I know. It sounds amazingly cheesy and really, even stupid, but I can tell you this simple habit – that costs nothing by the way – is incredibly effective to get people willing to open up to you. Honestly, for me an undesired and unintentional side effect of doing this, has been attention from members of the opposite sex. So, if you're having trouble in your love life, try this and I guarantee your troubles will be no more. But in terms of selling finance and insurance products, this will enable you to get the coldest of customers to start to warm up to you.

Next, you say your full name. You're not Joe, Steve, Nick, Rick, Anthony, Miles or Bob. You are your full name: Joe Sabatini – in my case anyway. You say your first and last name with an assertiveness and a smile. Shortly afterwards, you encourage your customer to make themselves comfortable and start asking them leading questions about how positive their purchase experience has been. Get people to talk and think positively any way you can even if you need to field concerns. It's important you do it before you start trying to sell them something rather than while you are trying to sell them something. Fielding their concerns does more to create a favorable impression of you and your dealership because it shows you care. Let me tell you, when people genuinely feel you care about them, they'll do just about anything you recommend.

"Are You Genuinely Enthusiastic and Glad to See Them?"

This may seem like the most basic of all basics, right? Well that's easy to dismiss as routine, but this fundamental mental state of the Business Manager is absolutely necessary to prevail and to give the best chances at succeeding with any particular customer. Why? How many salespeople come into your office and give you the "death look" of a "cash deal," or a customer that says "they don't want anything, I went over it with them!" It's unbelievable, isn't it? How about this one. "They're just wasting time!" The customer has completely sold the salesperson and they do a great job at attempting to sell you, not to even give it a shot. So, you know how you feel after a salesperson throws a load of junk on your desk, right? You feel like getting that deal jacket and throwing it at their head. Am I wrong? I know. I get it, I understand it. It's important to go through this in your head, but never, ever project negativity to the salesperson or the customer. Understand that if and when you allow the salesperson and/or customer to sell you on why they "don't need it," your job, your obligation is to put on your "A GAME" and with politeness and assertiveness, listen closely as to "why" they believe this. Listening is about 70% of the game; being prepared to overcome concerns and having the tools is the second part of success. Do not ever allow yourself to be convinced that you have "no shot." Even if you get convinced mentally, persist still. Undeterred, go after it and have faith in your persistent efforts; you'll surprise yourself!

I discovered that a customer only has so much tolerance to hold onto their predetermined "plans" in light of logical facts that help them close on something beneficial to them. Sometimes their wall of resistance collapses suddenly and they just say "yes;" oftentimes on that last ditch "Hail Mary" that I thought of not taking. Take the Hail Mary's, especially if you feel a little uncomfortable because the customer said "no" several times.

Treat every customer just as enthusiastically as the customer who is buying all the products. I've alluded to several ways of doing this, including smiling, looking them in the eye, saying or thinking "I really like you" under your breath, etc. An enthusiastic salesperson creates a situational force in which the customer feels mentally obliged to reciprocate an enthusiastically good decision to buy an extended service contract. Let's face it, there's not a human being alive who would not like a lifetime bumper to bumper warranty on something they purchase. Nobody in the world wants the onus on themselves to pay for unexpected mechanical failures. Therefore, contrary to the claims in Consumer Reports, extended warranties provide people with the security they desire – whether they admit it or not. I've never encountered a person who wants to pay for repairs. I'm begging someone to try and convince me that they would prefer to buy a brand new car with no warranty at all and save maybe $1,000 or so. Would anybody do that? If so, call me directly, we need to have a discussion. Truly, the chances are that a customer would spend the extra $1,000 and buy an alternative car that came with a warranty.

You need to bring this inherent knowledge with 100% of the customers you face and that knowledge will bring you the confidence time after time. So, make sure you do not listen to the negative salesperson, you do not carry the negative weight of the "No" you didn't even hear yet.

Let them tell you "No." When they do listen, ask "why," "why," "why," and then "why" again. Let them keep talking about it.

"Are you an Expert in Your Field?"

People will listen to what you have to say if you maintain that professional demeanor – no matter what happens. Some people – about 10% – 15% of them – will get offended by your persistence and you will need to be armed with the tools that logically diffuse them. With the closes that I will give you in Chapter VI, you will have the tools that will give you the confidence to look people in the eye and close. *That's* what an expert looks like. An expert is never emotional, fast eye blinking, nervous, shaky, etc. An expert knows, listens with intent and shows the customer that he/she cares no matter what and genuinely has an interest in getting the customer to see the things that you [the expert] NEED them to see! It is imperative that you see being an expert as your obligation to the customer – for their best interests!

In summary, never stop reading books, enjoying hobbies and learning to expand the tools necessary to be able to close. I got to where I am as a closer because of my curiosity, creativity and persistence in seeking the best ways to sell. I believe that nobody is "unsellable" and that sales are only lost by a couple of words not by a couple of dollars. Lost sales are opportunities to figure out what you can do better the next time and remember it, practice it in your head and finally test it out on customers. But never settle for: "There's nothing I could do." Understand that you will find the right road to the sale – even if you need to travel down all the wrong ones to find it by process of elimination. But you must be willing to travel them – it's the only way you'll discover the next level.

Most importantly, when a customer raises an objection, the professional demeanor demands that you stay open and understanding, so that the customer feels so comfortable that they have no problem telling you anything. This is the first part of selling at 90%! Always, look people in the eye, stay on their side – no matter how much effort it takes – and keep listening (ideally with a smile but at the very least with a look of endearing confidence in your position).

"The Bubble"

Being an expert also means getting out of the bubble. "The Bubble" is a mental place that gets created by our innate desire to try and find easy solutions to problems that are hard to address. Getting out of the bubble means being honest with yourself and addressing hard questions that have difficult – but possible – paths to improvement. The fastest identifier of the bubble is looking at your numbers and seeing stagnation. If you are not where you need to be, but you consistently miss and your attitude is negative, chances are you are in a bubble and the first step is identifying your mental block. The easiest way to identify your mental block is to humble yourself to constructive criticism, even plain old criticism. "Keep your friends close, but your enemies closer," from The Godfather, is a lasting quote because your enemies will gladly tell you where you are weak; they don't care about your feelings and I'm asking the reader, if you find yourself in this bubble, suspend your emotions to find someone who will be honest enough with you. You truly do owe this to yourself.

III

The Advantages of
"The Box" and
How to turn the
Disadvantages of
"The Box" into strengths

Ahhhh . . . The good old "Box!" Where all the fun happens . . . If you like being the brunt of the accounting office and Controller's issues, paperwork slaves to salespeople who tell the customer they'll be done in "just five minutes," contracts, credit card machine, fax machine, computer and customer complaints about "what's taking so long," the last one to leave when the asshole desk manager tells the salesperson to "spot it" at 9:01 and he gladly strolls out the door without a care in the world. Sound familiar? Oh, the beauty of a life lived in this hole! Let's face it, you feel kinda glued to the office, right? Yes, it sounds like I'm whining and I have to admit I am a little bit, but understand that it's only through this profound hate, loathing and disgust for being trapped in a hell hole of an office that I've discovered the greatest advantage. You know who else feels systematically stuck in "the box" when they are in it? *The customer*! You're probably asking yourself, "How is this possibly an advantage?" Read and remember this, especially all the rookies out there: **You have a captive audience! I have never ever ever had a customer get up and walk out of my office for any reason, for anything I said – no matter how much pressure I applied.** If you don't know me, ask around, they'll tell you I am an absolutely relentless, unforgiving, don't take "no" for an answer hammer (that's not a compliment because usually I like to sell with the "feather" whenever humanly possible). My point is, you better have the full confidence and mentality that nothing you ask these customers to buy will make them jump up and leave your office – I can assure you of that! The customer has already invested God knows how many hours into finding the right car, price, dealership and salesperson they want and they will not leave. Seriously, there've been times where I've purposely tried to make customers get out of my office so that they would leave. As a finance manager, you need to know that the customer feels systematically obliged to never get up – and they never will – so SELL, SELL, SELL, SELL! You know how much money advertisers would pay to have this captive audience? The customer literally has to hear what you are saying – it's your job to get them to listen. Do not allow yourself to get hurried for any reason, including the customer's request. You simply say: "Sir/Ma'am, I understand you are in a hurry and I assure you it's very important to me that I get you out of here as fast as possible. That being said, based on previous litigations in our state, my employer requires all of our customers to have access to this very important information for you to review for your own protection as our valuable consumer. Is that ok?" They are always going to say "Yes," and then proceed to go down the menu of contracts with them.

Before I get into the mechanics of Menu Selling in the Box, I would like to speak of something where I know a lot of Finance and Sales Departments fall needlessly short: getting the F and I manager out of the Box and getting the finance minds involved early and often. I've noticed at a lot of dealerships that I've worked at, visited and observed, the desk managers are really quick to strip away the rates, go to extended terms (even without the customer's request) and get into an array of "If I could, would you" closes. We can do much better than that! The problem has become that the profit motive at most organizations is falling second to volume – which is grossly ineffective for proper training, management and customer expectations.

Here's the good news. The Finance Managers still do, and always will, get paid on pure profit. Not only that, they have the knowledge to quote rates/terms and the Finance Manager has much more mental leverage as a negotiator than the desk manager (in these volume-based stores). Why? Because the customer cannot "smell the blood" on the Finance Manager. Any manager who has been through finance knows when to put on their "banker" role and give no tells of excitement, anxiety, fear of rejection, fear of customer walking. Truth is the Finance Manager doesn't want the deal unless he's making at least a certain amount of money. Also, the Finance Manager is the main source of bank negotiation as well. So, the Finance Manager can seem like he/she is conceding rate, but then may get a lower rate through the same lender due to the business relationship established. The Finance Manager should get involved in quoting payments and desking deals early and often, especially for people with scores below 680 because the expectations and variations are so great that a lot of profit can be gained by using multiple lender rates.

As a Finance Manager, you will need the support, trust and interdependence of your sales staff to reach extraordinary numbers. You need to incorporate yourself into the sales process, with the sales guys and desk managers, closing customers before they even reach the Box. Also, you will get higher penetrations, more satisfaction from the customer and you will get more profit on your products outside of the Box. You, as the Finance Manager, must make it incumbent upon yourself to go the extra mile to get on the trusting side of the customer as soon as possible to produce results. This alleviates some of the burden on the sales guys, which helps them relax and sell more smoothly. It also relaxes the customer, knowing the manager is involved and that they are dealing with an expert in their field. See how it all comes together? As much as possible, a Finance Manager should look at their office merely as place where they finalize deals and do admin busy work when they are not closing. I personally loathe being stuck in my office, so I take every opportunity to get out of it and make things happen!

So, in summary, getting extraordinary penetrations is not magic, guys and girls. Just get out there and be the one that the desk managers and sales people rely on, count on and trust to bring it on home for profitable and payable deals! Selling and closing deals is still a very instinctive game. Customers rely on body language feedback to determine how much they can keep pushing and when to say "yes." The customer will always say yes when you sell them that they are getting the best of everything, including professional and preferential treatment. Which means, not getting defensive, listening, making eye contact, paraphrasing back to them and affirming that you understand them; however, at times, saying "No" to them and still getting them to say "Yes" to a deal because they believe the deal is truly special. Everybody is walking around today with a sign – although at times it is hidden because they don't know who to trust – that says "Make me feel special!" Is it any wonder that the customers who feel the most special are also the ones who we've made the most money on? It happens for a reason, ladies and gentlemen. That reason is being prepared with the tools necessary to get into your customer's heart and mind. I've been in the car business for ten years and I know half of the people reading this are looking at that last part like: "There are so many assholes out there that just want to shop my number, waste my time and buy from the local competitor." That may be their plan, guys, but it's up to you to get them off auto pilot and start being their captain. You will not win all the time, but you'll love the challenge after you've succeeded several times.

Habits to Stay Away From

Another amazingly ridiculous process that I see a lot of Finance Managers do is put paperwork organization and processes in front of customer satisfaction by making the customers wait longer times while the manager gets his or her paperwork all neat, pretty and organized. I hope you're picking up on my facetious tone because it's the dumbest habit I've ever seen for a lot of reasons.

First and foremost, the time that elapses between when the customer agrees to a car deal and when they move on to the next step in the process is what I call the "black hole of negative consequences." That is when the customer starts second guessing, thinking with less emotion, checking their smartphones on whether or not they got the best deal. Also, their frustration about waiting time overtakes the excitement and anticipation of getting a new vehicle, which makes it less likely for the most positive outcome. The customer sees you – the Finance Manager – as the reason why this is "taking so long." You do not want to start off on the wrong foot if you don't have to. So back to my pretty little paperwork organizers, and "deal loaders," get that customer into your office as fast as possible! Why make them wait outside (and forget about formal interviews, more on that in a little bit). Fellow Finance Managers, you can find plenty of down time to organize your funding packets and state paperwork after the customer is gone. Just get the deal over with! It's funny, every mediocre Finance Manager I questioned says the same thing: "I just have to do it this way." Yeah? Well wouldn't you rather just be at $1,700 a copy? This seems fundamental but there are plenty of reasons to maximize the customer's time in the Box, rather than waiting to get in it for stupid reasons. Time is more valuable than organizational aptitude in the "customer waiting to get in the Box" situation.

Secondly, you want to maximize your captive audience time! Every second counts, especially with customers who continually say "No" to your service contract. In this case, working for time efficiency works in direct opposition to your goal to optimize opportunity and minimize the number of rejections you can possibly get. In other words, you want to be on the border of unnecessarily prolonging your time with customers. So, do not have your paperwork all nice and prepacked ready for the Accounting Department. You need to run unconscious interference on the customer that you need to work hard to upsell.

Lastly, the sooner the customer gets in your office, the more you can maximize your ability to find common ground with them and become more than just the "guy doing their paperwork."

To optimize your comfortability with bringing customers in earlier than when you're "supposed to" traditionally, you want to set your computer screen facing only you, without the customer gaining access to open visibility. This way you can set up your menu correctly and you can adjust prices with a concealed screen – and you minimize customer scrutiny while trying to optimize product revenue. If you are wondering, the answer is "yes," get the customers in the Box while loading their information.

IV

Menu Selling: Set Yourself Up for Profit Maximization

"It is by example – not opinion – that people begin to believe in themselves"
– Philip Zimbardo, The Lucifer Effect

Sales Floor Support and Desk Support

In a world full of average, small minded, small thinking, mediocre excuses, you have to be the leader by mastering the mindset of persuasive solutions, or in simple terms, keep coming up with other "great ideas" or "great alternatives" for the customer. Choices create an easier mind system for compromise and closing for both parties. You need to be the one who shows the sales guys not to give into the temptation of comfortable failure, comfortable path of least resistance selling, comfortable low gross deals. Bad habits and the easy way out are the unlocked doors to failing. You must be the "key" to unlocking the door to success. Do not marginalize the fact that "unlocking the door with the key to success" takes effort. This also means that you need to get the sales desk on your side.

I know I mentioned this before and I'm mentioning it again because you – as the Finance and Insurance Manager – need to create the situation among your staff to make the "back-end" (as we call it in the car business) as equally important as the "front end" (front gross profit on the car itself). This is not an easy battle at most stores but it's worth the concentrated effort. As F and I managers we're used to uphill battles anyway. Right? It takes time, patience and even maneuvering with sales management.

One of the most interesting phenomena of the car business is the heavy amount of Desk and General Managers who have no F and I experience whatsoever. In my opinion, being in finance should be a rite of passage from the sales floor to Sales Management because these guys have no idea how much profit they are missing out on! They literally have never learned the profitability "killer instinct." **Just because you do not see or observe something doesn't mean it's not there.**

Desk managers who have not done F and I do not know what they are not observing while closing, generally speaking, and because of that they do not know how to push the profit envelope as far as possible on every deal. What does this mean? Well, it's easy to justify forgoing $200 of profit on any given deal, right? Wrong! $200 x 200 units is $40,000 in gross profit – and believe me this is a very conservative number!

So how do we deal with this? Embrace a concept called ultimate accountability. In the Finance and Insurance position you need to leverage your conduit ability between the sales floor, sales management and the customers. Remember, only you (usually) know the rates, terms or approval, banks to use and proper book values. If people below you are taking short cuts, call them out on it professionally, and don't forget to get in touch with the human side of coaching. These sales guys want to be successful, chances are they're just used to some egomaniacal ass talking down to them and treating them as if they are substandard – no wonder why they never improve. Right? Be different! Believe in their ability to change their mind about strengthening their closing skills. Show them you believe in them and I promise you, you will have sales guys that insist on closing customers with products in the deal. If (peers) desk managers continually allow the sales guys to take the path of least resistance, again address it with the managers and volunteer your help. Volunteer to go close the customer with the knowledge that only you have.

Lastly, when Executive Management views F and I as the side plate, over time, you need to work on the system itself and produce results that will allow them to make a decision to enhance their view of finance profit. This can be done in several ways: enhance product portfolio, enhance salesperson and sales management pay plan and enhance finance pay plan.

In terms of product portfolio, a lot of dealerships are leaving money behind out of excessive product offerings, specifically tire and wheel, paint and fabric protection, key protection, paintless dent and windshield protection and etching protection. Just about everybody understands that the "main course" of ancillary products are the warranty and gap products and, for the foreseeable future, that's going to remain the same. That being said, most dealerships get penetration levels of the "other" ancillary products to a measly 10 – 20% at most! If you work at a dealership that has the tire and wheel, key, etc. on stand-alone policies you need to promote change in that arena and get the company to consider doing a "5 in 1 Plan;" wherein, all these "other products" combine into one big product with one cost and one sales close. This is cost effective for all departments; it gives considerably more value to the customer and the penetration possibilities on this kind of policy is through the roof – relatively speaking. Some of you know exactly what it's like presenting a menu with 8 different options – the customer's already mentally gone! Their attention span during the first go around is about 30-45 seconds, tops (and that's being generous) and with an 8 item menu it's nearly impossible to adequately and effectively give your dealership the most efficient opportunities to make the most profit.

In terms of pay plan, it makes sense for dealerships to get back to the fundamentals of general car salesperson behavior 101 and that is: "They're only going to do what they get paid to do!" This isn't the Salvation Army here! Sales guys will get creative if it makes them money, so it's imperative that the dealership incentivizes appropriately for after sale penetrations and profits. So many dealerships are making this fundamental error due to an error of being pennywise and dollar stupid and not realizing the potential for penetration levels – 60%! Hey, owners, how much extra money would you make if your paint and fabric protection or tire and wheel protection plans were at 60% rather than the industry average of 9%? Enough to pay your sales guys a percentage over the cost. Right? Right! So, fellow Finance Managers, get your owners and/or executive managers to wake up and smell the profit because not only is this a profit center, but it can also be a dealership differentiator in the marketplace.

I've worked at many stores; some F and I pay plans are "pot based" and others are based solely on what deals you get yourself. Dealerships that have the "eat what you kill" F and I pay plan are the most inefficient.

47

The Finance Managers turn to cherry picking fat deals, burning through cash deals, or just trying to find excuses not to do them at all, make customers come back with their bank draft already made out at a time when it won't be "their turn" and a whole creative arrangement of not maximizing profits on **every single deal possible.** Sound familiar? Owners, if you are also living in the bubble yourself and saying, "Not at my store (with pride)," get out of the bubble, because it is happening! Also, dealerships that incorporate the stand alone pay plan experience the highest level of Finance Management turnover – and that costs dealerships the most in re-training, re-hiring, etc. Why? Because, the Finance position is already hard enough, then you add the element of having Finance sharks in the tank looking to outmaneuver each other into getting the "fat deals" – which also does not increase closing skills, it just promotes backstabbing and angst.

The pot system alleviates a lot of the pressure that faces Finance Managers and allows them to focus on one thing only: closing the deal that's in front of them and creating an environment that fosters inter-dependent teamwork – and not individual greed. Can you imagine three Finance Managers all trying to work on closes and role playing together and out of intrinsic motivation to increase profits? Let's face it, we've all had those days when we get five bad cash deals in a row. Right? It just happens! But the good news on a pot system is that the other finance managers are getting the good ones and it's still helping you financially, so the Finance Manager never needs to worry about being a complimentary paper pusher and watching the other finance managers eat filet at the same time.

It is a fundamental human desire to associate with others; this creates the need to belong. In Finance, you need to be the control center of creating this need to belong from everybody. The people belong by participating in product sales and finance growth and it takes a daily effort to convey its utmost and vital importance to the dealership profitability. Make the dealership and the customers feel the need to belong to Finance Department growth as a requirement. Thus, the finance profit, product and growth should be a social event that binds the groups of interested parties together. In essence, this will overcome the whole nature of being scared to hit people with a number higher than where they said and capitalize on the fact that the vast majority of consumers intrinsically want to take the onus off of themselves for paying for unexpected, untimely and inconvenient repairs. I've been in the salesperson's shoes! I understand the mental wear and tear of closing a customer on the car itself. That's why the Finance Manager and desk manager need to be the fresh face, the tag team to ignore all the sales tactics the customer has been giving the salesperson on their desired, "beer payment for champagne dollar," car payment.

The Formal Interview: DO AWAY WITH THEM!

Every warranty contract company representative will tell you: "This is so important to penetration and profit." I completely disagree! The formal interview is a question and answer session that pretty much lets the customer know that you are going to try and sell them something and automatically puts the customer "on-guard" in my opinion. So, the situation is this: The customer just got done the process of committing to a huge investment and, in this day and age, the average customer invests 8 hours on the computer and usually another 3-5 hours picking out the car, negotiating and finalizing a payment of cash, financing or a combination of both. Now, some guy they never met before is asking them all sorts of questions about their driving habits, where they keep their car, how long do they keep their cars and if they've had any repairs done. Assuming the customer answers truthfully – which is a very loose assumption in a "formal interview" with the "Finance Guy" – chances are it's very awkward, the answers may take away from the closes I'm going to arm you with in Chapter 6, the customer often doesn't feel comfortable enough to establish rapport with you and most companies encourage you to try and get the paint and fabric protection as a closing question. Once you present a product, even if the customer says, "Yes," the customer is bound to firmly close and let's face it, no Finance Manager will have a job if they have a high closing percentage on a product that really does not drive business into the Service Department; nor does it encourage repeat and return buying habits of customers. Closing paint and fabric product and informally interviewing the customer for ancillary products should ideally be done by the salesperson before they get the car detailed.

Ladies and gentlemen, I completely agree with and encourage getting out of your comfort zones, but this is a futile and inefficient process built for the dinosaur ages of the 1980's car business. The representatives usually are not nearly as qualified as you are. They don't do deliveries on a regular basis, they don't know the stronger salespeople on the sales floor and they are on a corporate mission. You cannot take your career lead off somebody that has different goals than the dealership you're working for. This *does not* mean you do not listen to anything they say, especially if you are brand new to Finance. These guys (generally) still do have a great foundation of knowledge, skill and ability to make you comfortable closing product once you're in the box.

So, without the formal interview, what do you do? Keep it light! Primarily, your job is to get the customer to trust and be comfortable around you and you want them to see you the way they see their insurance agent ideally; friendly, not aggressive, professional, easy-going and most importantly human! It's a great idea to have things in your office that highlight the things that you love. Obviously, pictures of your family pull the heart strings immediately, but go bolder as well! Posters of your favorite band, sports players/teams, books that you have read or are currently reading. Also, having music playing in the background is great for setting your office as a place of promoting that easy feeling we're looking for. I know these things alone will not sell you anything, but you need to understand that a customer that feels positive is going to act the way you positively want them to. Oh, and owners, how about comfortable seats? You ever notice the metal chairs that are inherently uncomfortable in every showroom and Finance Office? Invest into seating that makes it harder for customers to want to stand up!

Secondly, load the deal while talking to them. The customer is going to feel like they are part of something exclusive. Why? Because every other time they've bought a car, the Finance Manager had all the pretty paperwork printed out and all the customer's information was already inputted in the dealerships "secret system" of confidentiality. I know I'm looking at this as though I'm dealing with the hardest possible customer and I hope you noticed that because you should anticipate and prepare professionally for the toughest, most detail oriented and nitpicky of customers. Remember, just about every other experience they've had in the business has already fallen way short by this point . Therefore, the customer already, relatively speaking, has more respect for you and what you have to say if you follow my advice to this point.

The essence of rapport is common ground, understanding and showing that you are caring. So, your initial conversation should start out with a formal and professional handshake, looking the customer in the eye and (whispering to yourself) "I love you." The customer will automatically smile and then you become friendly first, formal, mindful, considerate and maintain your professional demeanor while opening questions you would ask one of your best friends that you sit next to on a bar stool. "So what's going on? How's everything going? What brought you here? Is this your first time here?" Whatever comes naturally to you – this is the most important thing. The more relaxed and comfortable you are the more relaxed and comfortable the customer will react to you – 100% of the time. Also, keep it open ended, keep looking them in the eye with interest and care and allow them to keep talking. As a matter of fact, encourage it. Continue with statements like, "I agree with you. That must be great/ horrible, incredible, awesome/ painful/etc.; Tell me more about that. You know I feel the same way. I went through something very similar." I can tell you that most everybody can get hypnotized talking about themselves and the things they are interested in.This is a great thing because you're bringing out who that person really is and then they will do what they really feel like doing (not what they were instructed to do before another source made up their mind for them). This is not manipulation; this is genuine because let's face reality. Does anybody truly not want a warranty on their cars for as long as humanly possible? The answer is, not many people – the rare exceptions are the actuarial people and even then, they're not betting, they're not paying for the figuring out whether or not something will or will not go wrong. They're paying for the fact that, if and when it does, they won't be bothered with it at all as it relates to cost, inconvenience and disruption. So, when somebody sits in your office and starts to look at it as a "gamble" or risk assessment, they're already agreeing that they want the warranty. Why? Because they're already worrying about the risk and they haven't even driven the car off the lot yet.

In summary, remember that it's your job to genuinely want to make people feel special. Listen with care, be sharp as a tack, enthusiastic with a constant genuine smile and come off with confidence as an expert in your field – no matter what! I emphasize no matter what because you should realize that you were promoted to management for a reason: to be better than the salesperson in terms of talent and taking action, to always lead by example when a salesperson comes up to you and says, "They don't want anything." It is the hardest thing to do and that's why it's fundamentally important for you to know that only action will set the tone for change in your mood and that represents what will happen. You will be the change with action first. Always, will you look to act above and beyond what is "accepted" by everybody else as "fact" when a customer rejects your products and services. You sometimes have deals that the salesperson tainted negatively with the stubborn mindset of purposeful ignorance of that negativity and rejection. Assume that you're dealing with the typical "knee-jerk No" reaction and proceed to listen with intent to understand where they are coming from.

"Ultimate Accountability" is an internal mind-frame that accepts and understands that you – and you alone – are accountable for making things happen. Do not find excuses to not take action. Without action, all the greatness in the world can be theorized, hypothesized and conjured but nothing will happen without limitless action. Ultimate accountability through limitless action will guide you to find the correct answers to best practices and the truth is, most of you already know them! What to do now? Be the influential great that will change minds; create the circumstances that expose the best practices to your bosses and to your subordinates. People will follow by example and by results, and in the process, self-doubt will be systematically eliminated by acting before you have time to doubt the possibilities.

V

Step by Step F and I
Menu Presentation

Depending on which state you are conducting business in, there are various compliance laws that your dealership's Finance and Insurance Menu must follow. For those outside of the auto industry, chances are, you have unlimited ability regarding what you can and cannot show on your menu of contracts. These rules can include, but not be limited to, displaying the base monthly payment, the cost of each product being offered, the monthly payment, the interest rate being sold, the term, state fees, initial sales prices and trade allowances.

Ok, there you have it. The most optimal menu I've worked with ever. The warranty companies, financial services providers, salespeople and auto dealerships may want to listen to my work and words as the barometer because my company and I have produced record breaking product penetrations and profits. Consistently! My personal recommendation is a 3 to 4 contract item limit because a customer's attention span is only so long and companies want higher profits, higher penetrations. It's also scientifically proven that giving too many options can confuse an interested person out of buying anything. By contract item limit, I mean the individual products; so yes, a 4 product limit. While I understand that some people feel like a real hero when they sell Tire and Wheel, Paint and Fab, key replacement, etc. at full list to the 5% – 10% of the customers (this is the real average number of penetrations of standalone contracts at auto dealers) that see that much value in one protection of relatively minor setbacks and inconveniences, smarter organizations are committing to providing products of superior value to their customers.

The ultimate result is the invaluable satisfaction the customers feel when they use the product and that equals brand loyalty and that brand is *your* dealership.

Now, let's get closing, people! Prepare to gain confidence with the toughest of customer objections. To look at these closes only once would be a disservice to yourself, your employer and your family. Read them over and over, practice them on customers, paraphrase them; most importantly, make these closes your own with improvisational additions, your own facial expressions, body language, enthusiasm, excitement and conviction. Lastly, and most importantly (besides looking people in the eyes), *have fun with these closes*. Have fun with the customers, make light of all their nonsense objections and convert them with care in your heart. It will work when you put your head, your heart and your entire body into it. I think Vince Lombardi said something very similar, and it's crucial to engaging success, engaging fully outside of your comfort zone and stretching so that tomorrow you'll be an expert at what is alien to you today.

Below I will display what I believe to be the most effective menu I have ever worked with:

REPAYMENT CONTRACTS

ABC Toyota
Sale Price $12995
Base Payment: $258
Trade Allowance: $5000

Joe Smith
2012 Toyota Camry
Odometer: 40876
Last 6 of Vin: 888888

EXECUTIVE	DELUXE	PREFERRED
Vehicle Service Contract	**Vehicle Service Contract**	**Vehicle Service Contract**
8 YR/125,000 Miles	8 YR/125,000 Miles	8 YR/125,000 MILE
Pays for Parts, Labor, Diagnosis For covered repairs Towing and rentals included	Pays for Parts Labor, Diagnosis for covered repairs Towing and rentals included	Pays for Parts Labor Diagnosis for covered repairs Towing and rentals included
5 IN 1 TOTAL PROTECTION	**5 IN 1 TOTAL PROTECTION**	
Unlimited Claims For 5 Years	Unlimited Claims For 5 Years	
Tire and Wheel, Paintless Dent, Windshield	Tire and Wheel, Paintless Dent, Windshield	
Paint and Fabric, Key Replacement	Paint and Fabric, Key Replacement	
GAP INSURANCE		
Pays the difference between insurance Settelement and the balance of the loan If the vehicle is totaled due to fire, theft, etc		

Term	72	Term	72	Term	72
Interest Rate	6.64	Interest Rate	6.64	Interest Rate	6.64
Payment	374.50	Payment	362.74	Payment	344.55
BiWeekly Pmt	190.20	Biweekly Pmt	184.32	Biweekly Pmt	175.23
Biweekly Term	67mo	Biweekly Term	67mo	Biweekly Term	67mo
Term	75	Term	75	Term	75
Interest Rate	6.64	Interest Rate	6.64	Interest Rate	6.64
Payment	362.21	Payment	350.93	Payment	333.33
Biweekly Pmt	184.11	Biweekly Pmt	178.42	Biweekly Pmt	169.62
Biweekly Term	69mo	Biweekly Term	69mo	Biweekly Term	69mo

x_____
Customer Signature

x_____
Customer Signature

x_____
Customer Signature

61

VI

76 CLOSES

Preamble

Before I get started, fellow Finance, Insurance, car salesmen, aftermarket salesmen, retail store product specialists, trainers, entrepreneurs, etc., BANISH THE WORDS: "OPTIONS, WARRANTIES, ADDITIONAL PRODUCTS, YOU CAN DO THEM LATER, GUARANTEES" FROM YOUR VOCABULARY FOREVER! Do not ever make the customer think these are "options" about which they have a choice. Do not allow yourself to be sold on that idea because it's a disservice to you, your family and the customer. As I stated before, using logic, if the customer needs to think about it, that means they actually want the service contract because the customer doesn't want to have to think about it. That's the whole purpose of it. Read that last sentence again and again until the logic sinks in.

If you are selling ancillary products of any kind and you do not have *something in writing* that the customer can commit to and sign, then you are losing profit for no reason other than laziness because people need to see contracts and agreements in writing to feel more committed to opting in on it. You will notice some closes, or paragraphs within the close, will have the phrase "CATCH ALL CLOSE." These closes are the most versatile, strongest and my go to closes if I ever have trouble figuring out what to say next. Repeating yourself, though seemingly useless, does have a way of bringing the customer over the waterline needed so long as you remain confident.

1. **"The best sales presentations, are the presentations you don't have to make" Menu Presentation Close.**

   Menu presentations must be done 100% of the time. Most 2nd, 3rd and 4th close attempts will be based off a variation of the menu and the initial presentation of contracts.

   This close, on 1st attempt, will be used without seeming like you care if they buy or not. Your goal is to come off like their insurance agent, simply relaying information about their "Repayment Contracts." You will be enthusiastic, positive; however, your primary tone will be informative and you will not over dwell on the benefits on the first run through. Why? Because if you divulge all the benefits, people will lose their attention span and they are going to just go with their default, pre-determined answer without listening. Secondly, the people who already have their minds made up aren't listening much anyway, so why waste your best stuff when they aren't paying attention to it. Don't worry. You will get their attention!

   If you refer to the sample menu displayed at the end of Chapter V, you will use this on 100% of the retail customers, 100% of the time and you will always use the close below:

   "Mr. Smith, these are the contracts that we offer at ABC Toyota. I'll review them with you and then I'll get your state and financial paperwork completed in as little as 15 minutes; however, if you have questions, it may take a bit longer and that's quite alright, take as much time as you need. Is that ok?"

"OK."

"Great!"

"The 'Executive Contract' includes an 8 YR/125,000 BUMPER TO BUMPER Service Contract. It pays for all parts, labor, diagnostics at any [Specific Brand Name] dealership in the country, $0 deductible, includes roadside assistance and rentals when the car is in the shop so you're not inconvenienced.

"The second item is our exclusive protection plan, underwritten through [whatever major insurance company]. It is also $0 deductible and it covers all costs related to tire blow outs, wheel damage and even scuffs (very comprehensive), key replacement, paint-less dent removal, interior and exterior protection (to keep your car looking just like it does right now) and windshield cracks.

"The last item on the Executive contract is Gap insurance. Gap insurance will pay the difference between what you owe and what the car is worth, if and when the vehicle is deemed a total loss due to accidents, flood, fire etc.

"Your total monthly payment for the car and the addendums within this contract would be $374.50 at 72 months – or $190.20 biweekly; you'll pay the vehicle off in 66 months just by paying half every 2 weeks. If you wanted to do 75 months at the same rate your payment would be $362.21 per month or $184.11 bi weekly – you'll have the car paid off in 69 months that way.

"Now on the 'Deluxe' contract you'll forfeit the Gap addendum; see, the payments are lowered to $362 and $350 respectively, and lastly on the 'Preferred' contract you will be forfeiting the Gap and the Protection Plan addendums, your payments are $344 or $333 respectively.

"I see you're putting $5,000 down plus your trade, so I recommend the 'Deluxe' contract.

"Pick whichever contract you're comfortable with and I'll finish the rest of the paperwork."

This is the part when you shut up and study their eyes. Try to zone in on what part of the menu they're looking at.

2. **"Are/Aren't these Optional?" ["Emotional Deposit"] Close.**

No need to panic, ladies and gentlemen; this is a question that is a buying signal – though often confused by managers as a sign of rejection. As always, let the customer say "no," and do not assume that questions and concerns are negative responses.

Also, "emotional deposits" can be used at any time with customers. An emotional deposit is a statement that keeps the customer in an emotionally calm, comfortable and positive state of mind that promotes productive dialogue. The more productive the dialogue, the better chance you have of closing the deal. If the customer shuts down, or begins to shut down, the use of an "emotional deposit" can revive a person's spirit, mood and attitude towards you, the Finance Manager, and your contract offerings.

Emotional deposits are best built up ($50 per emotional deposit in the customer's mental bank account) – just like a bank account – because, make no mistake about it, you'll be taking emotional withdrawals when you try to close the customer 7, 8, 9, 10 or even 15 times! The better the rapport, the more you have a right to ask (withdraw $50 each time from customer's mental bank account). The more open ended questions you ask, the more the customers are considering it. Always do your best to maintain an interactive discussion. So here it is:

"Good question [emotional deposit]! Yes, they are, and I'm glad you brought that up too [emotional deposit #2] because while they are optional, the vehicle service contract is least expensive and the most comprehensive (covers the most) at time of sale. Also, it's much easier to pay an extra $30-$40 a month, get the best coverage for a discounted premium, and have the roadside assistance, than to pay the $2,500 or $3,500 it may cost to repair your car or buy the service contract a year or two from now. Does that make sense for you? The Deluxe contract really gives you the full protection from the time you drive off the lot."

At the exact same time, point to the signature line at the bottom of the 'Deluxe Contract' and say: "So which term makes most sense, the 72 or the 75 month contract? [Emotional withdrawal]"

3. **"No, I don't want any of these. Just the regular payment."**

Stay calm. Remember, this is a hard one because they haven't given you the reason, but you'll need to give them plenty of emotional deposits and simple questions to dig out the truth. With calm, cool, collective confidence look the customer in the eye and with body language that expresses genuine curiosity and concern:

"No problem at all, a lot of my customers say that. Why do you say that?"

Let them talk as long as they want. Do not interrupt them! Nod your head in agreement and try to find paraphrasing terms that show you understand their logic and then say,

"Why else?" Say why else and why else until they're all done.

The good news? They just gave you all the information you need to close the sale because you can use what they told you and offer your service contract as the solution that they need or should want based on what they told you. Never, at any point, should you butt heads with a customer because of the way they are thinking; it's your job to create the intrinsic value so that your product is a better solution for them than their "c – lawyers," or Consumer Reports or their own pre-conceived opinion.

This close is #3 because it's so important to never forget how to ask, "Why do you say that?" Other closes will be given based off the response to that question.

After they tell you, "Why," then you will select a close from below to pick from and give them an option.

4. The "Shut Down" Close.

Before I get into the closes where people are engaging you, I want to make a special space for the most difficult customers. The customers that sit there in silence and won't engage in conversation; they just keep saying no, nodding their head, etc.

These customers have a special place in my heart because without them, I would've never become so good at what I do; however, they are the least desirable when you have them. So, thank you! I call them mental mentors because they compelled me to do some serious thinking.

One of my favorites. Get ready to battle! This close is specifically for that customer who won't talk. You know why they won't talk most of the time? Because they're scared you're actually going to make sense. So, their way of protecting themselves – from doing something they really want to do (silly, isn't it?) – is hoping that their "wall" will just make you shut up. In this case, you need to take guesses until you get them to spill the beans out of agitation or a desire to shut you up – and they usually all do.

This close takes full advantage of your "captive audience." They will not get up and leave. I can promise you that. It's not happened to me once – even when I wanted it to happen quite frankly. This close requires persistence and getting comfortable with being uncomfortable because you don't know how the customer will respond and that's okay. You have a job to do and you must provide the best you can for your company, your family and the customers.

After the customer just sits there and keeps saying, "I just don't want it," or keeps nodding their head and being stubborn, ask these leading questions or guesses to evoke a response. Your tone should be like that of a detective who has just figured out the greatest mystery in the world: excited and enthusiastic.

5. **"I know what's going on and I get it. Let me guess. You bought one of these service contracts before and something wasn't covered. Right?"**

If they say "Yes," great! You just figured out why and you have an opportunity to connect and differentiate your contract or provide them with more suitable options. A lot of times customers buy contracts that aren't the best choice for them and consequently they experience mechanical failure after the mileage/ years expire. It's your job to provide the best possible coverage for them – even if it's more expensive because you don't want that to happen to them again.

The other way to overcome it is by talking about how the underwriter of your warranty is better. In this case, it's a definite advantage if you use Toyota, HondaCare, Mopar, Ford, etc. because it's factory backed and the customer already intrinsically trusts the brand name. If you are able to say, "Well, this is factory backed, and I'm sure that other warranty you bought was with a 3rd party provider. Correct?" this will give you an opportunity to earn their trust and close with brand name trust and differentiation.

If you're dealing with another company like Wells Fargo or Zurich, your job is to sell the value of that company. My way of going about it is to familiarize the customer with that company and sell the fact that it's good anywhere in the United States and that it was underwritten to exact factory specifications.

If the customer says, "No," great! Guess what you do now? Ask another question.

"Ok, what is it then?" This gets about 70% of the customers to engage in conversation because the customer already responded with, "No," so the customer now naturally feels the need to reciprocate in Q & A. Remember that a conversation that starts in disagreement has a chance to be converted into agreement; however, no conversation equals no chance. The moral is, get them talking – even if it's not positive, it's better than not talking at all.

If the customer says, "No" and continues to be evasive, what do you do now? Take another guess and another and another. The other guesses include:

"Let me guess. You read Consumer Reports. Right?"

"Ok, I get it, you've had plenty of Toyotas in the past and never had a problem. Right?"

"You have your own mechanic?"

"You've bought one of these before and it didn't work out for you?"

"Did you have a friend or family member tell you not to buy this?"

I can go on and on about what to guess, but when all else fails, default to **close #12 and/or #13** below. These closes almost always get people thinking!

Again, subsequent closes to follow (5 closes just from the example questions above), but it's also important to know – with certainty — that with each guess the customer will feel more and more compelled to reciprocate a response that will show their hand. Try as they may to hold it in, but the more persistent party always wins. In this case, it's a small victory just to get them to reveal their true objection.

6. "Consumer Reports" Close.

The customer admits, says, or brings into the office a Consumer Reports guide and starts going into a story about how Consumer Reports alleges that vehicle service contracts don't benefit buyers. These people, generally, are very statistically oriented so the best way to grab their attention is to counter with statistics and logic to back up your argument. Here is how this argument typically begins:

"Sir/Ma'am, I completely get it, a lot of my customers put their faith in Consumer Reports and it's easy to see why [emotional deposit]. I'm glad you've done your research and are interested in educating yourself about the industry. In the interest of that it's important that I inform you that Consumer Reports is greatly benefiting from consumer buying trends of the last decade. In the '90s and early 2000s, customers tended to keep their cars longer and longer; like 6,7 or even 8 to 10 years; nowadays, according to the NADA, customers are trading in every 3 to 4 years."

If you know that this customer is trading in a 3-4 year old car or they purchased a pre-owned car only 3 or 4 years ago, you just gained immense credibility and can be seen as an expert in your field.

"When consumers buy cars more often, guess whose subscriptions rise? You guessed it right: Consumer Reports! Guess who benefits most from those subscription rises? You guessed right again. And why are people trading in cars in 3 or 4 years? Because they don't want to worry about even the *possibility* of repairs that may occur after their factory coverage has expired. That being said, doesn't it make sense to give yourself the benefit of not having any worry about 'it' [repairs] for the entire time you're financing your car plus some additional for only $30 more a month?"

7. "Consumer Reports" Close # 2.

This is a close meant for the customer who thinks you're just trying to get their money out of their pockets. You know what I'm talking about, right? That customer who thinks that all salespeople are just trying to benefit themselves only and have no genuine regard for the customer's satisfaction. Or they can just be the cheapest person imaginable sitting in front of you. Either way, your goal is to get the customer to believe that the service contract will be a cost benefit regardless of whether they use it or not – which it is. It's imperative that you sell with the genuine belief that, in fact, the service contract is worth the cash spent on it, even if they don't use it and this is how it goes:

"You know what. A lot of my customers say the same thing! It's the reason you're buying the Honda, Toyota, Nissan, etc. Right? A lot of people don't think of it like this but, let's just say you never ever use it. Even if you never ever use it for anything, not even the roadside assistance, it's still worth the money."

Then pause momentarily with intent. I use these kinds of paradoxical sayings a lot in my closes because people love thinking of things differently. I genuinely believe they do – and once you get that curious look form the customer who says, "What the F are you talking about?" you know you have them right where you want and they are ready to be closed because you got them to listen to you and not the inner voice in their head that's telling them they shouldn't listen to you. Again, you must firmly believe that everyone truly does want the benefit of a service contract. I genuinely believe it and therefore, I feel good about insisting on the contract because it is always in the customer's best interest.

After the pause you explain:

"Let's say all this does is guarantee you keep the car for the full 7 years you plan on right now. More and more people have the plans to do that, but they never come to reality. Why does that happen? Because the first time people see a tire pressure sensor come on or a check engine light or other warning and wind up having to spend $600 to $800, they trade their cars in sooner because they know that feeling of 'what if,' after they've already put $800 into it. Doesn't it make sense to just pay $30 a month and know that, even if nothing at all happens, you're totally covered – even after your car is paid off? So, let's take that over the course of a lifetime. Instead of every 3-4 years like you've been buying, you keep cars 5 – 6 years, the actual terms of your loans . . . [this is the big close] **If the only thing this service contract does is ensure you keep** your car for 6 years instead of the 3-4, like most Americans, you'll save hundreds and thousands of dollars over the next 20-30 years."

8. **"I never buy any of these warranties" Close.**

Catch All Close.

The best line of attack for this one is very simple, and yet a lot of Finance Managers allow themselves to get sold by customers. The key to this close is taking steps. Don't get all caught up in the moment, the customer's disdain, the customer's body language and agitation. You simply need to ask:

"Why do you say that?"

OR

9. **"What makes you say that?"**

The differences are subtle but some Finance Managers and sales people are more comfortable with saying "What" rather than "Why." Saying "What" tends to keep people's defenses lower for some reason.

Understand when the customer is saying "no" in an agitated and unfriendly manner, they are remembering something that happened to them that bothered them for some reason so please make allowances for that. They don't hate you, they're just aggravated at something or somebody else that happened in the past. Usually it's not you.

If they respond, think 'Great!' Their response will probably be something like:

"I have just never used them," or "When I bought one before the item wasn't covered," or "I'm not going to keep the car for a long time," or "I'm buying a Toyota, " etc. Do you see how all of these closes are starting to come together now? You can mix and match them, but most importantly make them your own, combine them and you'll see the common questions and closing signals.

If they don't respond, guess what their other option is? To shut down! In which case you refer to the Shutdown Close – **Closes #4 and #5.**

10. **"Maybe you're right, maybe this coverage isn't right for you" Close.**

What? You really expect me to say that? Yes. I do! It works great especially after you've asked them, "Why is that?" It's great because this loosens the customer up to actually being a human being due to the fact that you are relating to them. You follow this up with:

"If it's okay with you, discuss what experiences and research have led you to that possible conclusion. So, what was it a friend, mechanic, etc.?"

It's important to put forth suggestions because it automatically evokes the customer to reciprocate in a Q & A, which ultimately leads to a sale.

Close Number #11 is a great close – or at least – a great way of differentiating between whether the customer has a "concern" or an "objection." They're very similar but it's important for us sales people to know that a concern is much easier and simpler to overcome and close #11, pretty much handles the concern that a lot of customers have, given the overwhelming skeptical, genuinely fraudulent TV ads and other information abundantly available, regarding the integrity of the product you're offering and proceeds to close if the customer really does want a warranty intrinsically. It capitalizes on the opportunity to not go back and forth in which case, you can effectively make the most profit. More back and forth means more chance of negotiation in the finance office.

This close is just a reminder that you don't need to bring a hammer to something that only requires a feather to close.

11. **No, I'm buying A Honda, Toyota, Nissan [Brand Name]. This is a reliable car, isn't it? Are you telling me that I'm buying a piece of junk?**

Gotta love the customer who gets smart. Right? Actually, you do. The customer that tries to keep you from insisting on a warranty is the most scared! Do not back off when you hear objections or are "mocked" by the customer and proceed to *get on their side*, instead of against them, with this close:

"Not a problem at all, Mr./Mrs. Customer, I need you to understand that this is not a warranty like those you see on TV. This is a service contract that is factory backed (or replicated to be factory backed) and gives you the exact same coverage as you get from the initial 3 year/36,000 mile warranty. So, I really think you should at least go with the 'Preferred Contract'."

Point the pen to the line which is dotted and if they start looking at it, great news, you have a buyer! It's just a matter of negotiating at that point.

12. After #11 Close: "It fixes your car when it's not even broken" Close.

Catch all close

Obviously, you can use any of these closes whenever you feel it's going to be effective, but after you go through Close #11 is when this one is particularly ideal, because you can assume the customer is saying "No" because they really believe they don't need a service contract. It's a genuine objection and not just a concern.

So, you now know the customer is objecting and it's not just a concern and after they say "No" or some other negative response, you then use:

"Mr. Customer, I understand and if I were you I'd feel the same way too; however, what this does – this Preferred Service Contract – is it fixes your car when it's not even broken."

Again, brief pause with intent, study their body language if you can, but 9 out of 10 times they're going to give you that dumbfounded look or come right out and say, "Well, what do you mean by that?"

And then you begin to explain: "Sir, you can still drive your car with a check engine light on. You can still drive your car with a tire pressure monitoring sensor going off, or traction control sensor, or air conditioner not working, back up camera, Bluetooth, sunroof, etc. ... You can still drive your car and these things are broken and most people do in fact drive around with these things broken because they want to believe it's nothing, but in fact they could be doing even more **consequential** damage. Doesn't it make sense to have a rental car, a network of any Toyota Dealership in the country, 24/7 roadside with the preferred package for $30 a month?"

This close becomes a lot more effective when you are aware of the exact equipment that the customer has in the vehicle they're buying; like Rear DVD player, NAVI, Bluetooth, Heated Seats, Power Seats because then they actually envision these things failing – as they have in the past.

Again, always point to the contract and the desired payment you recommend.

13. The Vanity Close: "You owe it to yourself to reconsider it" Close.

Catch all close

This close can be used as a preamble or "pre-close" to another close or used on its own. I find it best used as a preamble to #12, but I have used it by itself. You will need to feel out the situation yourself. **This is my favorite close** because it gets the customer's attention immediately and it makes them listen to what you're going to say next. So, just imagine how effective it would be to say this:

"I know you said you don't want the Preferred Contract, but you really owe it to yourself to reconsider because of what this does; it fixes your car when it's not even broken." See how I'm combining them?

If you don't use it as a preamble in the above example, then just use it as a standalone and reinforce your initial menu presentation benefits:

"You really owe it to yourself to reconsider – at the very least – the preferred contract because it will keep you covered, $0 deductible, roadside assistance, everything in the brochure, instead of having to pay out of pocket for the last 3 – 5 years of your loan."

Think about it. Some people take out 72-75 month loans on cars that have 0 years or 1 year bumper to bumper coverage on used cars! INSANE, RIGHT?

14. Group Associations/Labels/Stats Close.

This close takes full advantage of the fact that people are more likely to do something when they feel that most people do it. This is best used before a recommendation or after an objection.

"About 80% of our customers at ABC Honda take at least the preferred contract because they have used it and they repeat buying due to how efficient it is for our customers' time management and convenience – at a network of every Honda dealer and ASE certified mechanic in the country – when there is a covered repair."

This close can also be used when somebody is close, they've said no and they just need that little extra motivation:

"Sir, you owe it to yourself to do the preferred contract. I mean seriously, our figures for last year showed that around 80% of our non-leasing customers bought – at least – the service contract."

15. The "I have AAA/USAA/GEICO Roadside Assistance already" Close #1

Customers who are leaning toward opting out tend to cling to any part of the service contract that they feel isn't a real value. Understanding this is paramount to closing the customer because they're essentially saying that they intrinsically value everything else about it; all you need to do is get them to see value in the one part that they used as an out:

"Oh, thanks for bringing that up, a lot of our AAA members who are customers say the same thing, which is why it's important for me to ask how much do you pay for that coverage per year?"

"Around $100 or so."

"Ok great, our service contract will not only do what AAA does, but it will also pay for all repairs related to mechanical failure, pay for a rental and reimburse you if you're on a trip. So, this contract is just a bit more and instead of only getting the 5-mile tow that comes with AAA, this contract will tow your vehicle up to 150 miles! Which means if you're in Philly, you blow a tire just outside of New York City, you get your car towed back to Philly!

And AAA won't cover any repairs for when your car's not even broken! Labor itself is $115.00 per hour!"

After you get them to see value in the perk of the vehicle service agreement that they previously objected to, you then proceed to embellish on the aspects of the vehicle service contract that they value and close.

See again, how I'm mixing and matching?

16. **The "I have AAA/USAA/GEICO Roadside Assistance already" Close #2**

"That's great. Hey, what's your policy number? With AAA – as a member you get a 15% discount! So, that would bring the preferred contract down to $322 a month and you'll be covered up to 125,000 miles bumper to bumper, parts, labor and diagnostics included!"

You then – as always – use your pen and point to the dotted line. Some people will still say they don't need it because they have towing coverage already. In which case, you clarify two important things (if they don't spit out another true objection or question):

a.   Are they objecting because there's some other reason that they really don't want it?

b. Are they objecting because they feel that they're paying for double coverage? If they are objecting due to the perception of double coverage, then you look back at **#15 or**

17. **Just say directly: "Cancel it because you get far more for your money. With our service contract, they not only tow your car, they also pay for rental and repairs."**

    Not every close has to be complicated. Some of the best closes are just direct rebuttals said with confidence!

    If they're objecting because they don't want it, you can find out by assuming that they're objecting because they have double coverage, and then proceed into:

18. **The "I have AAA/USAA/GEICO Roadside Assistance already" Close #3**

    "I hear you, you're paying 120 some odd dollars a year for this coverage. Right? Look at it this way: Take that number and multiply it by 8. That's $960 and all they're doing is towing your car. For just a little bit more you can get even better roadside assistance benefits, a free rental for when your car is in the shop and all the computers, electronics, windshield wiper motors, door locks, back up camera, etc. covered for 125,000 miles, parts, labor and diagnostics! AAA gives us this discount because they cannot tow on highways in most states as well. So, for just a couple of extra dollars a day, you're getting a far better deal."

You then use your pen, point to the line which is dotted and look them in the eye.

I also want to point out here that we got through 12 different closes before we even mentioned a discount. How about that. Twelve different ways of working the customer in seamlessly effective ways and the one thing we didn't discuss was discounts!

19. "I can't afford it" Close.

This objection – or concern – is one of the most common you'll hear, especially when you have a customer who was dealing with one of your weaker salespeople; the type who never plants the seeds of products because they're scared. As if the customer is suddenly going to back out of the deal because a product was offered. Or a salesperson who pretty much got manhandled by the consumer and did a great job making the customer overzealous and thereby stuck at the payment they were closed at.

Just to see if this is the true objection, without blinking an eye and with great concern: "That's exactly why you should get it because think about it: If you take your base payment and then you have – well let's just say you have our average warranty repair cost – last month our average warranty repair order cost was just under $1,500. So, what would your monthly payment be without the preferred contract if this occurred? $255 + $1,500 = $1,755 and then after that you're still self-insuring don't forget, so if something else occurs – like another $1,500 repair – then guess who's on the hook again?

"Whereas, with the preferred contract, after something happens and gets fixed – for free by the way – you're still covered." Point to the line that is dotted, look the customer in the eyes and say, "That makes sense, doesn't it?"

20. "I don't keep my cars that long" Close.

It's very important to treat this literally at first. The customer may be saying they don't intend to keep the car for all 8 years. So, the first line of understanding is to find out how genuine the concern/objections is:

"I understand, you have a 5 year loan, so are you saying you plan to keep it for the length of the loan or may want to keep it a year or 2 after that?"

If they say any time frame more than the factory comprehensive coverage, then you just proceed to close on what they told you; so, let's assume they say the length of the loan only:

"You know, I'm glad you told me that [emotional deposit], so if you just double up the 3 year/36,000 mile warranty to a 6 year/75,000 mile warranty, I can do the Deluxe Contract, giving you the benefits of the full protection provided by both amendments, for the same price as the Preferred Contract or the Preferred Contract will be only $319 for 72 months: Which do you prefer to go with?"

21. **Every close has the common element of preparation of different contract options immediately ready! The more prepared you are to handle objections as minor roadblocks – with different contract options as the solution – the more effective your closing percentage will be. Being prepared, in and of itself is a close.**

We're 21 closes in and I need to remind the readers of the importance of preparation. Preparation is a close within itself because preparation leads to immediacy, efficiency and contributes to the consumer's perception of your credibility as an expert. If you are prepared with solutions for your customer, you are an expert. Options – although we never say the word "options" in front of the customer – lead to decision making.

That being said, you need to have at least two vehicle service contract options ready to roll right off your tongue at all times, in front of all customers.

You need to be prepared for the regular mileage driver, the low mileage driver and the high mileage driver and adjust your playbook accordingly AT THE DROP OF A DIME. Remember the importance of being perceived as sharp as a tack!

Always remember that closes are to be used like an expanding and contracting muscle. Sometimes, you need to retreat until you gain more rapport or find out information that may seem unrelated to them, or possibly they'll just warm up to you as the proximity of "the box" almost guarantees if you maintain a positive attitude.

22. The Dealership Commitment Close.

The close is best used for the customer that is on the edge or just believes that you are trying to make a dollar off them for the sake of it; in other words, the customer who thinks you are vain.

This is also best used with some sort of commitment letter from the dealership that the customer is obligated to sign as part of the dealership's compliance package. This form can be used as another closing tool after the customer has already said "No" several times.

You put the paper in front of the customer and you say.

"The owners of our dealership strongly believe in ONLY products that have the ability to deliver you value. I know you've already said 'No' several times, but the owners know that customers who do at least the Preferred Contract are more than twice as likely to come back to our dealership to buy a car. The reason is because when you need to make a claim on this vehicle service contract, you will remember that our dealership had staff that cared enough to insist on making sure you're protected. You know the feeling you'll have. Right? That feeling will pretty much guarantee you'll only buy a car from us."

Again, you then pull the menu in front of them, point to the line and ask for their signature.

23. Fundamental Close.

As part of the "close/retreat" aspect of closing in the box, you must remember to never put your menu away. Your menu is always the FUNDAMENTAL INSTRUMENT to the close of the contract you want them to have. So, during your times of retreat, you either turn it over or you move it to the side to see if the customer's eyes wander to view it while you're processing state paperwork. I recommend turning it over for the customers who are close to shutting down because you want them to believe you're done selling, while they are proceeding to sign other paperwork because then they'll allow you to gain rapport comfortably and then you can close. The people who seem to be unsure, but say, "No" on the first go around, should have the menu kept in front of them.

Use your state paperwork as a buffer between closes. Have a certain order PREPARED for the *toughest customers*. I would always start out with odometer statements and power of attorney forms. On used cars, I would also have them sign the Carfax and the Federal Buyers Guide, before they see the menu – again, I like the element of surprise and the time to feel the customer's vibe. Think about it this way: How the hell would you feel if some stiff suit you just shook hands with asked you for $6,000 in product? RAPPORT, RAPPORT, RAPPORT. Earn the right to ask for the sale an unlimited number of times.

24. "I'm a gambler/ I'm betting on this car" Close.

This is for the customer who has confidence in their product, but if you logically listen to this close, you'll hear doubt inherent in anything in life. Right? Think about the customer that says "I like to gamble." No, they don't. That's a facade and an attempt to sell you. Do not go down without insisting on this principle:

"You know what, I do too. I think that's great! Do you like thinking about your bets because you're going to be thinking about this one for six years. Sir/ Ma'am, you see this has nothing to do with gambling and everything to do with – simply – not having to worry about your bet. Either way you're a winner. Doesn't it make sense that if you're thinking about this as a gamble, that you don't want to be thinking about it? You see, you're not betting for something to go wrong and I'm not betting that something won't. What I am doing though is making sure that either way you win!"

If the customer just gives you a stupid look like you have five heads, then get your menu and ask for the signature on the line that is dotted.

If they ask you, "Well, how's that?" you already have them; just go into the "Even if you never use it" close and/or remind them that:

25. **"You're paying for this because you don't want to THINK about whether or not you'll NEED to use it. If you're already thinking it's a tossup now, you're already a person who doesn't need another thing to *think* about."**

26. **"99.9%" Close**

This close is for the customer that thinks that the car they're buying is good enough not to need a warranty. A very common objection. This is a great 2nd or 3rd close after the initial menu presentation.

"I know, I have a Toyota myself. I agree they're great cars and I'm sure yours will last for a long, long time.

"But think about it this way, your factory [or certified] warranty covers over 5,000 parts, most of which are moving. So, if your car were 99.9% issue free over the next 7 years, that would be a standard of success. Right?

"Great! So, that still leaves 5 parts that you can expect to fail over the course of that time and THIS CONTRACT WOULD COVER ALL 5 of those parts! Our average warranty repair order – and that's the average repair order; some are higher, some are lower – is $1,400! That's a lot of potential savings! So, we should do the preferred contract?"

If you still get a "No"...

27. "99.95%" Close

"OK, let's, just say that your car is 99.95% reliable, that's still 3 parts. Doing the math of self-insuring, that's $4,200 just in parts, labor and diagnostics, let alone the inconvenience, towing, etc. Doesn't it make sense then to do the Preferred Contract?"

28. The logic close – If you were the Motor Company, would you predict more mechanical errors in the first 3 years of operation or the 2nd 3 years?

These closes are thought provoking. They get the customer thinking about the basis of why they are saying they don't want a warranty. And once they really think about it logically, with insight, they usually prefer to opt for it. These thought provoking closes are best used in tandem with other closes. Remember to always end with a leading question to a close.

29. Logic Close #2

"Mr./Mrs. Customer, if this car [brand new/certified used/used car with factory warranty remaining] had no warranty on it, would you even still buy it?"

If they say. "No," then you know they intrinsically – and without thought – have just placed an extremely high dollar amount on a warranty because they just said the car was essentially not worth buying if they had to bear the financial responsibility of unexpected repairs during the first year to three years.

If they say, "Yes," then you say, "Great!"

30. *How much less* would this vehicle you're purchasing be worth then?

Hopefully, they're upfront with you and usually the answer is around $1,500 – $2,000.

"Great! This vehicle service contract I'm offering you is around the same amount of money for an extended period of coverage – well beyond the limits of what's included in the price you are paying for it. I'll just need your signature right here."

Sometimes the customer won't give you an answer. In that case you, put forth the $1,500 – $2,000 just to move the conversation along in an agreeable manner and 9 out of 10 times they just go along with what you're saying. I've never heard the customer say that they would "pay the same exact price for the car;" that statement would defy logic.

31. "Don't say 'No' just because you think you 'know' what you wanted to do before you got in here."

You can shorten this one up to just, "Don't say 'No' because you think you 'know.'" This is obviously a play on words and you have to be careful on the tone you use with this one. Obviously, the rapport being built is paramount to the effectiveness of using this close in tandem with being light hearted, yet honestly assertive while you say it.

Again, on this one they're going to look at you funny and then you'll follow it up with your reasoning, regardless of what they say:

32. "You ever do that before? You know, when you have your mind made up regardless of what new information and sensible reasoning somebody that cared about you gave, but you still went ahead in another direction out of strong will? But then

later, you say to yourself, "Why the hell didn't I just listen?" At 75 months, it's only a few dollars to make sure that doesn't happen."

And/or:

33. "I've never heard one customer come in and curse me up and down in regret about buying this; however, I have had plenty of people say, 'Joe, I wish I had listened to you'."

34. "The Storyteller" Close.

This close is very important and is most effective if used in conjunction with some of the other closes previously mentioned; particularly the, "This fixes your car when it's not even broken" close.

The world is addicted to stories – both fictional and non-fictional – you can be assured that most will listen to a good story about a warranty claim. My story went something like this [after using whatever close I felt most appropriate]:

"For example, when I took my Dodge Challenger in for the tire pressure monitoring sensor, the local Dodge dealership used my Toyota Warranty. I showed them the number to call because they weren't used to using Toyota Warranty claims; they called, had to order the part and sent me

on my way. If I didn't have the warranty it would've been $1,400 – and my car wasn't even broken!"

So, within that story I used 3 or 4 different closes, I would get really into the story too, like I would talk about the dealership I went to, walking in the glass doors, the service manager's name, the color of the walls, how I felt when my item was covered and how easy it was to use for me.

35. "Storyteller Close #2"

This is one of my least favorite to use; however, in some cases it really hits home for people who don't want to listen to positivity. As much as I hate to admit it, there are a substantial number of people who have the most active, ever present and dominating pity party daily in their minds. The only way to get through to somebody who is saying, "No," to you and has this negative mindset is to play right into it. How do you do that? Tell a story that puts them smack dead in the middle of the story that leaves them in a powerless situation without a service contract:

"I've seen people making car payments who are right in their budget and then have a repair of over $1,000; just imagine what that feels like? You know what happens to your stomach when you see that check engine light! All of a sudden

the questions come up; you go into denial; you say to yourself 'it's no big deal;' maybe it is maybe it isn't. In any event, what most people do is keep driving on it because they don't want to be bothered with it and then they cause something called 'consequential damage.' Consequential damage occurs when you continue to drive and then other mechanical problems occur because you continue to drive on it. In other words, your $1,000 problem just turned into $3,000 or $4,000! With this service agreement, as soon as that light comes on, you bring it in, no questions asked and you never have to feel like you're caught between a rock and a hard place or, even worse, the unknown and dreaded check engine light!"

36. Always point to the bottom line of the contract that you want them to purchase after you make a closing statement and say:

"This is the contract that would most benefit you and it's [this much] per month."

This is a fundamental HABIT that you need to execute. Always, focus on the monthly payment whenever possible.

37. "Which position do you prefer to be in: Making a choice because you want to or making a choice because you have to?" Close.

Again, this is a play on words, this will get interest because people will naturally try to understand exactly what you're saying. A lot of people really do have a natural yearning to comprehend and when you make statements that need to be thought about, you gain attention instantly and encourage dialogue. Once the customer is engaging you in dialogue you have a good chance.

But the substance of the argument is right now you have a preferential choice, the customer is in a great position, but that position can and will change eventually. Right now, they can buy the service contract for the cheapest amount, nothing is wrong with the car, it's freshly inspected by the shop and warranty repairs actually do occur! So, when they do occur, do you want to make a decision of trading it in too soon or paying out of pocket to repair it – either way it's costing them money and those are for minor repairs such as diagnostics, bearings, calipers, suspension, etc.

38. **"Let's say you fix the repair. *You know* mentally you're going to be burdened with the worry of what if it happens again and if/when it does happen again, you will most certainly be looking for answers from somebody. The truth is there's only one person who needs to be looked at for answers."**

The answer is themselves, in case you didn't pick up on that. Why?

39. **Because cars – no matter what brand – are not perfect [You can harp on the 99.9% close again at any time during this]! So, if your car has 3-4 problems out of the parts that make it up, this really isn't something out of the ordinary.**

40. **"Back it up with Stats" Close.**

It is a major benefit when you can provide the customer with stats that they can perceive as factually sound and logical:

"According to JD Power and Associates, the per capita for the number of Toyotas that have a warranty claim in the first 3 years or 36 months is 6 per 100 – so that's 6% in the warranty period.

41. **"So, if you had your choice, would you take your warranty in the first 3 years or the second 3 years of ownership?"**

This close asks a logical question to which you already know the answer. Of course, people would prefer the warranty at a higher mileage and after years of ownership because also according to the same study, **warranty claims quadruple in the following three years.**

42. Explain the warranty cost like a life insurance policy close.

Every now and again, you get the person who defies logic and reasoning and decides to say something like, "If anything goes wrong it'll happen in the first couple of years," so obviously, #38 would work perfectly, but also, most people have a life insurance policy, so you can make it a point to explain why the rates of the warranty are cheapest now and why the coverages and the cost goes up as the car ages – just like a human being **for a life insurance policy. The price goes up based on the risk for age.**

43. "Don't put so much pressure on me" Close.

This close is great for the customer who asks for a huge discount OR (and especially for) the customer who tries to come in your office and act like they own the dealership. You guys know the type, right? The ones that tell you, "Let's move on" or "Hurry up."

I insist on getting at least five "No's" from every customer. It must be a habit of every successful Finance Manager who wants to become great. Do not let yourself off easy because then you'll start having inconsistent penetrations.

This close is great when the customer says, "Moving on."

You say, "**Please, stop putting so much pressure on me [say it with a lighthearted tone]! I have an obligation to my dealership and your family to insist that you listen [pull out the menu], and also state law requires that our dealership gives you full disclosure because what happens a lot – more often than you think – customers, and lawyers who represent their customers, call up and say, 'What?'"**

Ask the question. This is a very important part of the close because you get your audience to engage.

Customer says, "They say they weren't offered it."

You say, "Right! Don't you want to be part of the group of people who don't have to get involved in that sort of carrying on just because you didn't want to spend an extra couple dollars a month?"

44. "The Reality." Close.

Catch all close

This is an excellent close. This close is great for the customer who feels they need to be just as adamant about saying "No" as you are about getting them to say, "Yes." Some people think there's always an agenda to "screw" them or otherwise "gip" them out of money. So, this is a great way of being "real" with them. You must strongly endorse your products, be passionate and enthusiastic to pull this close off. This close works best after you've tried several closes and you don't feel you're getting anywhere. It's also great to use when somebody is trying to blow you off or along with a discount to your product.

45. **You could even come right out and say, "I love your personality. I really would be saying 'No,' just because you want me to say 'Yes' too. But you really should listen because of what this does: it fixes your car when it's not even broken!**

You need to be very careful with these closes. You must have a light heart with these folks because usually this close is for people who will not allow you to build rapport with them after you've tried (because they're scared of doing something that will benefit them). Crazy, isn't it?

"Mr. Customer, I know you think that I'm this salesperson just trying to sell you anything to make a dime and I get it. If I were you, I'd be saying the same thing and the truth is, you're right! It does benefit me when you purchase this warranty or this Gap insurance. But also, I've seen what happens when people give me the 'Don't I have this coverage' call."

46. **"You want to know what the 'Don't I have this coverage' call is?" Or how about the**

47. 'Nobody offered me that warranty' call?"

"I get these calls at least once a day. Some situations are worse than others, *but I've had people who needed engines replaced and they had to foot the bill themselves; in which case, they immediately trade the cars in afterwards – can you guess why?* Sometimes people really can't afford it because they're on a tight budget and they are really in a bad position because of it. Again, I'm being real with you when I say, you owe it to yourself to have the preferred contract. Sign here."

Most people truly are on a tight budget, so this will strike a nerve. Be confident, keep going after it! Specific examples of people's situations help tremendously.

"I just got off the phone with a guy today, put no money down on a Honda Pilot. His insurance check was $2,500 short. Guess what he didn't buy? Gap. Guess what he had to do to keep his credit unstained? Mr. Customer, you're financing 110% of the vehicle value plus taxes and tags, God forbid something happens, you will have to pay $3,000 out of pocket – or you can pay $10 a month!"

48. "Close in 30 Seconds."

Catchy, isn't it? This close is another one that can be used best on people who come in completely shut down and are aggressively shutting you down. The customer who insists on insisting they don't need to even hear about the coverage. Also, this close can be used if you've tried to close the customer so many times that they're just not even paying attention – this can happen from time to time, don't be discouraged.

With this close there is not time for pleasant exchange or emotional deposits. This customer just needs to be hit assertively, looked in the eyes with confidence and assurance.

"Mrs. Customer, give me 30 seconds to speak because you may be glad that I insisted; however, if you're not then we can just hang up this conversation. Is that fair?"

Sometimes customers are just scared of listening and they put their defenses up in an aggressive manner to defend themselves. So, the best defense for them is to not discuss it.

This is a great lead in to be used with any other close you feel appropriate.

49. "Don't hold yourself back from taking action that you should take" Close.

Just say it like it's written, people. The entire logic is that you're going to get them to do something they know is for their benefit. Not yours.

So, what is holding them back?

The answer lies in emotions. The different end to this close is:

50. "Don't hold yourself back from taking action that you should take because you're emotional. Let's think about this logically, not emotionally. Does that sound fair?"

And then you go through the most logical closes in a step by step manner:

Would you like knowing that for the whole term of your loan, you'll never have an additional $1,000-$5,000 expense?

Can you afford the payment with the warranty?

Great! The preferred contract, sign right here.

51. "Stuck on think about it" Close.

"Mr./Mrs. Customer, I can see you've done a lot in your life and you've made plenty of decisions that required action. That being said, I'm sure never in your life have you let this nominal of an amount of money prevent you from really standing between what you really wanted. It's obvious that you understand and agree with this: The preferred package really is the best option for you. Did you want to extend the term to 75 months or keep it at 72?"

This close is of best use for the person who you know is close and you know they want to find a reason to do it; however, they feel like telling you they want to think about it because they are mentally stuck at a payment or cash sale figure or told themselves they wouldn't do it before they stepped into your office.

52. "An ounce of charm for a pound of profit" Close.

This close is a great lead in/combo close. A lot of times, after a customer silences you one, two or even three times, you will need to find new creative ways to approach your guest in a way that doesn't seem to infringe on your respect for them.

"I know you've made your decision, however, I have to tell you, the pleasure of having the ability to cover your vehicle really, sincerely, is a privilege that you owe to yourself to have. Really, it would be my honor for you to give me 30 seconds of your attention to let me tell you how this contract fixes your car when it's not even broken."

If they still won't let you speak then just come right out and say,

53. "With all due respect, it's not my intention to infringe on the tremendous level of respect I have for you. If I were you, I would be acting the same way and it's important for me to let you know that 90% of our customers go with the preferred contract after they listen."

OR:

54. "I may have insulted you because I'm honest in my genuine insistence, but let me be brave enough to apologize so we can move forward and make the most effective use of our time right now."

This close must be used with confidence, looking the customer in the eye and use of the hands to show openness and understanding. This close is great for getting people to listen.

55. "Need time to think about it" Close.

This close is specifically for the customer who says verbatim: "I need time." Listen carefully. Take it literally and close it literally:

"Mr./Mrs. Customer, I understand and I would think the same thing if I were you. In fact, a lot of my customers feel the same way because you really feel you're going to address this issue with the passage of time; however, life happens and then the very time you need right now, will work against you."

56. "You'll make a decision in the midst of a problem rather than listening to my solution which is priced the lowest – with the best coverage – right now!

"My point is you really don't need time to think about it, what you have here is a strong reason to use your time the most effectively and efficiently possible!"

57. "Because having the preferred contract is better than self-insuring" Close.

This close is a reminder to remember the simple less complex closes too, and to ALWAYS enhance the use of the word "because." Because customer behavior is always drawn to the end of the sentence. When you hear "because," even if you're only mildly interested in something, you ever notice how you are naturally drawn to pay closer attention to what the person is saying?

This close is most effective when somebody is engaging in conversation, however, not closing.

58. Another Brick in the Simple Close.

"You think you don't want to say 'yes,' but logically, you do! C'mon!"

Be careful with this one. Rapport is paramount when delivering this in a lighthearted, but serious manner. It's crucial to laugh with the customer when you say this one.

This close is effective because it's so simple and it gets the customer to,

59. **"Stop taking life so seriously will you! This is good for you! This is a way better decision than eating *a double quarter pounder from McDonalds*."**

Not only is this close simple, but it also gets people to laugh at the same time, getting them to realize, that this will not hurt them and,

60. **"This decision may be good for me but it's great for you."**

An inverse to this close is,

61. **"Just because this contract is good for our organization doesn't mean it's bad for you; it's quite the opposite."**

This close is best for the customer who insists that you're just trying to make a profit off of them for the sake of it.

62. **"The Strongest 'I need to think about it' Close Ever Written."**

"It's better to take a deal that you know is better than you ever expected right now [pause] than to wake up tomorrow [OR WHATEVER TIME FRAME THEY SAY THEY NEED] knowing that you missed the opportunity."

This close can be used to sell the car itself or the warranty or anything you're selling when you know the customer is close but is noncommittal. These customers usually never walk through the showroom again, they never return phone calls because the bottom line is there was something about the sizzle of the deal that wasn't there. It's up to you, the Finance Manager or salesperson, to create that sizzle and the call to act "now" because later will never happen.

The customer may proceed to give you one of those insanely annoying lines like,

"If it's meant to be it will be."

This is a genuine sign that either the car is not right or the price is not.

63. **"[Customer's first name], I know you've obviously done a lot of great things in your life and I know that every great – or at least very good – decision you've ever made in your life was made using the exact opposite approach, so how about I give you the employee deal now. I'll give you the preferred**

contract at 72 months for the lower (75-month payment).

64. "Then you'd have to do the deal today. Right?"

Now, we're getting into the discounting closes. I know in the fantasy world of closers we'd like to say that we never discount, but fortunately, we're selling items that can be replaced relatively easily and we're not emotionally attached to inventory, are we?

65. "The Ghost of Christmas Future" Prefix Close.

This close is prefix that can be used as an add-on to just about any of these other closes or used by itself. This close needs to be used with sincerity, assertiveness, and kind of lighthearted laughter.

"I know you think this is just a sales pitch, but this is not just a sales pitch. These are stories that come true and we see them play out every day. These are facts."

This is also for that customer who you know deep down inside won't do it because they aren't in the mood to be "sold" something. This happens often. Even when logic, facts and their own gut wants to say yes, but they still won't, use this close to get you over the top.

If you're selling cars and you hear that customer who really wants that particular used car that you know will be sold tomorrow, this is the type of pressure they need.

66. "Is this deal good until tomorrow?" Close.

This close is for the person that is specifically looking to stall making a decision, despite your best efforts to exhaust ALL other rational and logical reasons to make a decision. These people must have pressure applied to them. You *must believe that closing them is a service that benefits them* to pull off this close with conviction.

So, the customer asks the above question and you say, assertively, positively and with a lighthearted tone . . . a smile on the face helps too:

"Mr./Mrs. Customer (first name), absolutely not! Because this deal, at these numbers, is so generous; the best in the country. So, if you're not certain at these numbers – the best and *most special numbers – then I don't even know what I'm doing! Probably just because it's important to me that you feel extra special* – then you'll never be certain. In order for me to justify these numbers to my boss, I need you to take this deal right now because I will not do this deal five minutes from now."

Combine this with close #62 for a great combo!

This is a strong close. It will force your customers to step up because they truly believe that they will not get a better deal anywhere else.

Some people may get offended because they feel you're applying too much pressure on them. That's ok. Just stay positive. Most of the time when this happens they'll say something like,

67. "I know what you're trying to do" Close

Immediately and without hesitation, just fire back: "You do. I'm glad you do! Because what I'm trying to do is make you take advantage of a deal like I would give to my own brother or mother and make the most efficient use of your time. Do you really want to be doing this again, at another dealership or down the line, another four hours? According to NADA, consumers go to 1.4 dealerships; which means that most people buy at the first place they go to if they feel they are treated fairly and transparently with the numbers – as we have. You do not need to go to another source to figure out what the majority of the buyers in the market are telling you. We are #1 for a reason!

"Doesn't that make sense! So, let's just do the preferred contract at 75 months, sign here."

These closes are lethal on cars or service contracts because the option is the same: "They want to think about it" (which may or may not even be true) and you (obviously) don't want them to. Ladies and Gentlemen, sales is about getting as much as you can, while you can and when you can. The moment the customer leaves, your time may mean nothing, mine as well, so do EVERYTHING within reason to do a service for your customer.

Also, selling the contracts at the same time as the car is usually the most profitable for the dealership. In other words, presenting payments for the car and the warranties at the same time all the time is the best way to grow retail profit per unit.

The purpose of closes #66 and #67 is at some point, you need to separate from trying to understand WHY the customer won't do it. By the time you exhaust all attempts to gain understanding, even if the reason actually exists, they're not going to give it up. Time to zig zag around it to the close.

Always, always, always **try to make a call to immediate action, immediately after you make a closing statement. Do not just leave the close up in the air.**

68. SPIKE them down with a call to "sign."

Mentally visualize it just like that: A volleyball team setting up, leaving the logic-ball up high in the air (close) and spiking (call to immediate action right now).

VII

Keeping Credibility While Closing on a Discount

Discount closes can make a great complement when used in conjunction with previous closes. It does not hurt to repeat previous closes at the same time as you discount. For example:

"You really owe it to yourself to consider the preferred contract, especially if I do it for only $15 more a month."

It takes away the plain old – "if I could, would you," that people are so used to. Don't get me wrong, it's fundamentally the same; however, you're still focusing on value. The discount is just an additional bonus privilege that they are receiving.

First thing to remember:

69. **Ideally, and there's a big emphasis on "ideally," discounting should be done only after you use and exhaust at least five other closes before you get into discounting AND**

70. **Discounting should be done systematically in at least three tiers.**

Catch-all method

YOU ALWAYS ASK A PREDETERMINED Suggested Retail Price [1st **Tier**]. I don't care if they are paying cash or if the salesman says, "They don't want anything," or whatever other predetermined fear that exists in the realm of the unknown that makes you want to get weak and offer them $200 over cost to start. Price does not sell contracts. But the sizzle of selling the value of the deal, relative to a high price, usually will! It is incredibly important to leverage the relative starting price and payment with your 2nd, 3rd or even 4th offering of a discount. Your initial offering should always be at least – and I emphasize at least – $1,000 of profit on a vehicle service contract.

Your **2nd Tier** of discounting should usually be anywhere from 20% – 35% of your markup depending on level of interest and the customer's level of comfort with you.

The **3rd Tier** should be $200-$300 over cost.

Finally, the **4th Tier** should be $1 over cost to $100 over. I can just hear a bunch of old school car guys now calling me weak and I know, I get it, but the bottom line is these warranties have an unlimited supply and you're creating the demand. Also, the dealership greatly benefits from the sale of service contracts. We all understand that gross is first, but never forget that synergy, momentum and penetration are a very, very close 2nd because it's good for confidence, morale and obtaining your goal. We'll also talk about getting on the "bell curve" in the next chapter.

With each tier, you should be using the above closes repeatedly to drive your point home. Repetition works! Pay attention to customer pauses after you drop a close. Also, pay attention to the closes that prompt questions and keep using them over and over again until you get yourself above the "yes" waterline. A lot of work goes into getting above that line – *always* persist.

Undoubtedly, there will be times when you need to get right to the point and take your chances at giving everything you have, or skipping a tier of discounting. Always try to leave yourself at least three tiers though because, sometimes, that last $100 means the difference with another round of closing engagement.

The tier system takes advantage of the fact that a customer only has so much resistance to something they're inclined to really want. In other words, you need to leverage the number of times you ask for the close as much as possible to get the best results. So, discounting needs to be done in an expanding and contracting manner and you should always look to maximize the number of attempts to close.

71. **Exaggerate the discount payment and the "special" of the deal.**

   Catch-all method

in simple terms, when you give the customer a payment on any contract that is $500 less, turn on your best and certain acting skills and close with how "unbelievably great" the deal is for them – so much so that you may think you're coming off as disingenuous. You may think you are, but this usually sells the sizzle and makes the customer believe they better do this deal because they are in fact "special." Also, it's a great time to speak about how many people buy the service contracts. People feel better – believe it or not – when they know everybody else is doing something.

72. Discounting Rate and Keeping Credibility – "The Modifier."

This close is very important! You must hold your ground if a customer tries to become overzealous and force you into giving them a better buy rate without the service contract. Simply tell them "No." Even if the customer goes from hot on buying the warranty to aggravated; hold your ground, do some other paperwork to pass the time and take another shot at selling it. Don't ever forget the importance of the "expand and contract" mechanism to closing sales on warranties.

First thing in a rate discount close is to present it in a professional manner that showcases your expertise. How do you do this? Not by just throwing it out there by saying, "How about if I get you a 4.49 rate instead of the 5.49 rate, would you do it?" It's an attempt, but the customer will most certainly smell the blood of the discount gods if you present it like that and ask, "Well, why can't I get that rate anyway?"

Never ever use "rate discount" again! From now on relabel it to a "rate modifier."

Regardless of what you're selling, it's never called a discount on your front end profit or back end financing. This close is all about the feel for the customer; if you want to make the customer feel good about the decision, but every other method isn't striking a nerve, most people can logically put together the close:

73. **"Great news, Mr./Mrs. Customer, I looked through my various approvals and I was able to get you a rate modifier down to 3.99% making your payment the same for 66 months or only $12 more a month for 60 months, which option do you prefer?**

If the customer starts asking questions as to, "Why would the bank offer this?" explain:

74. **"The way the bank sees a service contract is less risk for them. You see, if you have a warranty for the length of the loan the chances of you defaulting or slow paying the bank goes down statistically. Does the 66 months make better sense for you?"**

Some other customers will proceed to press and ask, "What will my payments be without it?" Do not slip up and do not get shy. Quote the payments without the warranty at the initial rate they were closed on. Remember it is not against any law to sell the rate; however, if it makes sense for profitability to give a customer a $200 profit discount in rate to make $1,000 profit or even break even on a warranty profit offset, then give the customer the benefit, but never lose money.

Another question a customer may ask is, "Why wasn't I given this rate to begin with?"

This question can be handled in several different ways, but the best way is to come full circle with the "modifier" and "qualifier" label:

75. **"Great question! I'd be wondering the same thing if I were you: The reason is because you only qualify for the rate modifier if you go with the preferred contract for protection. So, does the 60 month contract work? Or the 66 months?"**

76. **"Up sell the upsell close."**

   Catchall close

There's a reason I saved this one for last. This close is The Hulk of profit maximization and product penetrations and it works all the time. Refer all the way back to the sample menu and recall the other contracts: the Deluxe and the Premium. Once you get a customer to commit to the Preferred or the Deluxe, this close will get them to buy another product package. This must be done methodically as to cement in stone the contract they already said "Yes" to. A lot of people don't try upselling the up sale because they have this fear that the customer will suddenly change their mind, especially if you went through a long verbal exchange. I get it! But I also know how to get you over. This is how:

For example, upon customer agreement to the "Preferred Contract" (especially if it took several attempts to close it), you have them sign the line on the bottom of that contract and then you turn the menu over. Proceed to do some state paperwork or disclosures of some sort in the interim and then readdress the menu:

"Mr./Mrs. Customer, I know you see value in the Preferred contract and for only $15 extra per month you can do the Deluxe Contract which includes the protection plan for your tires and wheels and pretty much everything else that isn't covered under the service contract. Essentially, you'll be paying an extra $15 a month to keep your car looking like it does today for the next five years. I just need your ok, right here or you can do it for the same payment at 75 months. Which do you prefer?"

BONUS CLOSE:

I should charge $50.00 for this close alone, that's how great this close is! This close needs to be genuine to be used effectively, and you must look your customer in the eye. You must care about your business and the organization you work for enough to make this work.

"How many times do you look back on your life and say, 'I didn't plan on this or that, but now – when you think about how your life has progressed – now, you wouldn't want it any other way?' Every one of my best customer relationships has started out just like this, now I'm asking you: Even though you are telling yourself you're uncertain because you didn't plan on this, I'm so confident this is the right decision for you, that you and your family will buy 10 more cars from me and this dealership. And I'm sure you will look back on it and decide 'you wouldn't want to have it any other way!'"

This close is powerful when dealing with uncertainty in customers. This close is a call on customers to make good decisions, despite their plans and what they told themselves they weren't going to do before they walked in. So many customers get really attached to a game plan before they even walked in, just to "think about things" and still wind up making a far worse decision for themselves and their families. Oftentimes in life, when something feels right logically, but emotionally we're overloaded, we tend to hesitate. This close draws upon real-life examples of how to keep decisions in life as simple as possible, but no simpler.

VIII

Mentality, Focus and Repetition of the Closer

How to Use Memory to Build Confidence

Your memory can be your strongest asset to continuous learning. Your memory should serve as the vehicle to guide you through unsuccessful attempts to sell and create opportunity to make future attempts profitable and successful. Make a habit of dwelling on the details of a customer you were close with and didn't sell, then pull out your notepad and keep your emotions out of it.

1. Write down exactly what he or she said.

2. What was the customer's pace and were you able to adapt to meet their needs?

3. What could you have done better?

4. What hurdle did you fail to get over?

It's important to define and remember what they said and what they meant. You should strive to always make sure that the customer knows that you understand them and what they are thinking. Once a customer knows they are being validated and accepted, the customer begins to trust you and feel comfortable and this is usually where most sales are lost and found. So, if your notes indicate that the customer didn't seem to understand you or you didn't understand them, then that means you were unable to gain the foundation of understanding that is necessary to get the customer to listen to you.

That leads me to the second question you should reflect on: Was the customer initially hurried and therefore, not open to discussion regarding contracts? If so, were you able to slow them down? This question is where a lot of Finance Managers decide to blame their sales staff and management. Great! Now that you've got someone to blame, do you feel any better about it? Probably not, so let's just focus on what YOU can do when it happens again – and it will at "Every Dealer/Retail Store USA" so you may as well sharpen your tools to perform your best. THESE CUSTOMERS CAN BE SLOWED DOWN ENOUGH TO SPEND MORE MONEY! It's important to remember, they do not have to be slowed down to the level of your liking, per se, but they need only to be slowed down enough to give you a solid opportunity to close.

Thirdly, in retrospect what is it you could have done or said based on what the customer said and how long you had them in your office? Are you able to remember what the true objection was? Did you feel you got enough "No's"? Most business managers get uncomfortable after the 3rd or 4th negative answer; it's vitally important to your success to take the uncomfortable shots or the one "last" shot before you give up. As the great Winston Churchill said: "Never, never, never give up."

Lastly, be honest with your self-assessment of where you failed and use your memory to profit in the future. Do not use your memory to beat yourself up and dwell on how you failed, rather, see the seed of tomorrow's success in today's learning experience. It's very important to use your memory in this manner. The daily rigor of the finance job and rejection will test you enough; do not waste your time over-exerting your memory, but do continue to focus on the principle that those who persist will succeed. ALWAYS!

Reading the Customer's Body Language/Type and leading with "Emotional Credits."

In the car business (or any business in which there needs to be a salesperson), a salesperson's ability to read his customer is vitally important to knowing what to say and how to say it as relates to which closes will work best. Each and every customer has a certain threshold that they will accept or report you to the owner because they're offended and it's your job to thread the needle and ride the line of taking "No" for an answer or being considered a bully and dealing with the unwanted consequences of that. Again, gaining a customer's trust, rapport and confidence in your ability as an expert makes it highly unlikely that the customer will be dissatisfied with persistence.

As a Finance Manager, I will emphasize the importance of using your pen on the menu and making constant eye contact with your client in front of you. Do not deny what you see from the customer's body language; embrace all of it, even if it's negative, and adapt your style, particularly your tone. Below, I will reference four general consumer styles that make it easier for you to get the client in front of you to say "Yes."

1. **Fast-paced, Direct and Assertive** — These people tend to make **quick decisions**, but they can also **quickly change their minds**. They focus on business and **don't really care about rapport** relatively speaking. These people are not heavily detail oriented but they will pay attention to big claims like "Fully covered, labor, diagnostics and parts and $0 deductible." Do not get caught up in going over your impressive memorization skills about every single nut and bolt that is covered with this type of person; you'll lose them and lose them fast. Do not let these qualities throw you off your game because they **come off as hard to sell**, but really, they just need to be hit with your fastest fast ball right up front and usually, they'll at least listen.

2. **Outgoing, Social and Upbeat** — These clients **are easy to get excited**; however, they can be very definitive when they make up **their final decision**. They like to **talk a lot**, so definitely rely on building rapport. These types can also come off as egotistical, so make sure you feed that if you can and identify with it as well. So, if a customer says they're so proud of their kid for being the head chess master, you better tell them how lucky they are to have such a gifted child and come off as genuine. The customer **can interrupt and ask a lot of questions**. It's important to stay positive, as these people will **also fail to pick up details**. Failing to pick up details can break a sale because, again, they may not hear you when you say $0 deductible the first time or

that it covers parts and labor or that no money ever comes out of your pocket or (believe it or not) that the car will be covered for a certain amount of mileage, like 125,000 miles**! Repetition is key with every customer** because a lot of times the customer is listening to themselves and just letting you run through your job, but they're listening to their preconceived thoughts.

3. **Thoughtful, Harmonious and Empathetic** — These customers **do not like conflict**, but they may also **fail to assert difficult questions**. These customers are most likely to be soft spoken. On its face, you would say these are the perfect customers. When they are leaning towards products, yes you're right. When they are not, you'd better be sensitive in your approach or they will shut down or lose profit at very least. These customers may be leaning towards your product, but you may have to guess about what questions they may have because they will be reserved.

4. **Logical, Accurate and Questioning** — I wish every customer had a little bit of this in them because these customers will almost always engage in your closes and remember, if you have a customer engaged in a conversation, you have a shot. The drawback is these customers **need lots of details to make a decision.** These customers are most likely to be the **"think about its."** You may feel that the customer wants **too much info**. Lastly, these customers may seem

134

uncomfortable socially. Again, do not be thrown off by their analysis or their display of suspicion on your offerings.

I admit I kind of tricked the reader because guess what: these four customer types are also four salesperson types! So, read through them for the common pitfalls that you may fall into or that you see hard working salespeople fall into. Most commonly, the logical salesperson: You know what I'm talking about, right? The salesperson who knows every technical thing about the car but the customer is yawning and you wonder why the salesperson sells two cars a month? That's a salesperson who is not in touch with his customers and thinks everybody thinks like he/she does! How about the salesperson who is outgoing and social, but fails to pick up on the details of what the customer wants?

In any event, before you can get the customer to buy a contract, you must get them to buy into genuinely listening to your pitch. Once they actually start listening, you can close!

Emotional Credits and Withdrawals

Customers have an emotional bank account when dealing with salespeople. This is one of the most often overlooked aspects of sales. If you fill the customer (bank account) with deposits you can take withdrawals without getting yourself into hot water with the customer. My point is: it is about rapport. More importantly, it's about making the customer feel like they're in control and that no matter what they're making the right decision **with** you.

My first time using this emotional deposits/ withdrawals approach was a solidifying moment because it absolutely gets customers to do what you want them to do while giving them nothing – except reassurance that you'll do whatever they want; however, you're going to do it on your terms and your timeframe (not theirs).

I was working as a salesperson on the Main Line and a Greek immigrant pulled on the lot, didn't even park his car, he had his Consumer Reports printout and he said, "What's the best price you have on this car!" I could see that he was in a hyper state, though more just wanting to get something done than confrontational, but I could tell he would've gotten confrontational TO THE POINT OF TAKING CONTROL OF THE SALE IF I WASN'T PREPARED.

I replied, "Sir, every one of my customers wants the best deal and I will get that for you as soon as I make sure we have exactly what you want in stock! By the way, I'm Joe. Welcome into . . . . Honda, glad to meet you. Thanks for stopping in. What's your name?"

"George," he said.

"Great name. Follow me. I have the CR-V EX right here. Is this exactly how you want it equipped?"

"Yes, but I want the best price (pointing to his Consumer Reports guide)."

"Not a problem, I wouldn't expect you to buy it if the number wasn't fair and affordable to you; however (withdrawal), if it's the wrong car then the price doesn't matter. Now you're looking to potentially spend over $20,000 with us, you deserve the best treatment and I'm going to make sure that you're sure of the car and the price," I said.

"Yes! What's your best price," he insisted yet again.

I said, "George, if I were you I'd want the same *exact* thing, brother. I assure you after we drive the car, I will get with my manager and work out an employee type deal with you! Fair enough?"

Finally, I got, "Ok, I'll park my car."

The rest was history. I gave him $500 off MSRP plus the accessories. He never questioned the rate and bought a warranty. This happens on car lots every day; however, the outcome is usually way different. The outcome is usually the salesperson trading in his suit and tie for a waiter's uniform and becoming an order taker because he doesn't have the tools to assert himself politely while not losing the customer altogether.

Rejections and emotional credits/withdrawals in the finance office work the same way. When a customer says, "No, I'm not interested in any of that," you lead in with some sort of emotional deposit.Normally I like to make sure I get two deposits for one withdrawal: "Mr. or Mrs. Customer, on my car payment I want the lowest possible payment too (deposit). If I were you, I'd feel the same way (deposit), most of my customers think just like you do too (deposit); however, if you have a $1,200 repair in the first year, then your monthly payment is really $100 higher a month and then you still don't have coverage (withdrawal). You owe it to yourself to do at least the Preferred Contract."

Other emotional deposits can be done before closing such as compliments to the customer, expressing to them that they're in control with phrases like, "Not a problem at all, but...I would be glad to, but... You're the boss, without you I don't have a job, but..." These are all ways of disarming the customer before you.

I can give endless examples of compliments, including the kinds of watches people wear, the handbags women carry, the T-shirts with the person's favorite band on it, their children's great behavior, activities and hobbies they enjoy that you enjoy too, etc. By the way, most women are flattered when you compliment the brand and style of their handbag and their outfits. Always remember compliments are free and they are a sure way to get off on the right foot with somebody you just met; who knows, you may even get one in return.

The Mentality of the Closer

One of the most obvious things you'll notice about the style of these closes is they take passion. They take the desire to be on fire! You need to visualize yourself getting into new things and conquering. It's part of the Philadelphia Style to hit things head on and make people awestruck by the tenacity with which we live. We are cut from this cloth born of influences like Rocky, Frank Rizzo, the Broad Street Bullies, and the Veterans Stadium crowds that can put fear in any opposing team. It's not to say that we as Philadelphians are bullies, but we will persist passionately until we cannot persist anymore. As the book draws to a close, let me quote the Philadelphia Flyers Stanley Cup winning team's Head Coach Fred Shero (1974-75; 1975-76): "To avoid criticism: Say Nothing. Do Nothing. Be Nothing."

This quote sets my ass on fire every day! As a matter of fact, it's probably gotten me fired from several jobs. Now, I'm not encouraging people to find reasons to get themselves fired if they are not reasons; however, I am suggesting that you should respect yourself enough to challenge systems that do not produce profit. You should be so successful that people think, "you must be doing something else." You should let your bosses know what works best for building profitability and most of all, you should not be scared of the limelight you will be in once you put these closes to use! People will criticize you. People will try to say you're doing something. Well, guess what losers focus on the most? Winners! Jealousy on the part of other less competent, lazy and average people has gotten me in hot water because I take risks: 90% of them are good and sometimes I should've held back. Professionals call these times that risks were taken "learning experiences," not mistakes. So, when you have a mediocre boss, with a mediocre ass-kissing staff of loyal sheep, what happens to a guy who stands out? Guess what I say to all of them now? "Thank you! Thank you for making sure that I didn't tolerate an environment where nothing is ever gained or lost. Thank you for firing me so I can keep moving up in life."

The Closer will see people that achieve and become believers! They will not doubt these successful people who constantly pull the world together for themselves and make it look easy. The Closer will watch and ask questions and learn. The Closer does not see and hear things and say, "I don't believe it!" If you see things with your own eyes, why immediately turn to doubt? Imagine, then, how hard it will be for people to believe you if they have not seen what and how you do it? The Closer acknowledges fear until that fear can be dealt with productively, because the only reason we fear anything is if we're unsure of if/how we can best it. Right? Replace fear with faith and confidence in your action in the direction of your desired path and you will see it!

Lastly, and in closing, the Closer will keep the open mind of a child. Constantly learning and undeterred from failures! The Closer will never get comfortable saying, "it is, what it is." *IT IS WHAT YOU MAKE IT!*

Author Bio

Joseph has worked in the Automobile industry since 2005, starting off at a Kia dealership in Springfield, Delaware County making just over $30,000 his first year. Since then, Joseph has become highly proficient in the training, practice, and closes necessary to compete and dominate in the selling of Automobiles, Vehicle Service Agreement Contracts and Aftermarket Product Sales as a Sales Person, New Car Sales Manager, General Sales Manager and Finance and Insurance Manager at various Honda and Toyota dealerships in the Philadelphia area. Throughout his career he has brought success and results that even his employers thought "will never happen," or "impossible" to dealerships where he's worked. Joseph has consistently risen to the top of every sales floor and over performed in every market he's been a part of in the Automobile business. Joseph graduated Magna Cum Laude from Peirce College in 2009 while working 50 hours a week selling cars. Before entering the Automobile industry, Joseph worked as a Correctional Officer at Delaware County Prison. He was also in Law Enforcement as an Undercover Officer after graduating from Delaware County Community College.

All proceeds from the sale of this book will be donated to The Middle Class Scholarship and Medical Fund. Since 2009, The Middle-Class Scholarship and Medical Fund has donated thousands of dollars to families of men and women in the car business for medical and educational purposes. Purchasing this book is not only an investment in yourself, but you are also saying "I'm there for you" to your fellow brethren in this business who deal with illnesses and hardships and still come to work day in and day out.

Contact Information for reaching Joe:
sabo2081@gmail.com
https://www.facebook.com/joe.sabatini3
http://linkedin.com/in/joseph-sabatini-a79a00123

One on One as well as group training available for Finance, Sales Managers and Salespeople.